This Book Belongs To

_____

Passport

Purpose

Journeys of Self-Discovery

led by Jeannine LaSovage, Martha Toth & Serina Brown of

MICHIGAN REACH OUT

Photos & Graphics by Valerie Toth, Martha Toth, Linda Salesky, Anne Mayer, Jesse Karnes, Mollie VanDerBos, Darius Dixon, Alice Wright & Beth Pepper

Mill City Press, Inc.
212 3rd Avenue North, Suite 290
Minneapolis, MN 55401
612.455.2294
www.millcitypublishing.com

ISBN-13: 978-1-937600-39-6
LCCN: 2011939628

Printed in the United States of America

Photo & Graphic Credits

Martha Toth: title page, 8, 31, 48, 54, 56, 57, 63, 64, 80, 98, 108, 109, 120, 142, 153, 157, 159
Valerie Toth: cover, 6, 24, 29, 38, 66, 71, 83, 86, 88, 104, 116, 126, 127, 130, 132
Linda Salesky: page facing 1, 3, 58, 66, 73, 76, 136, 145
Anne Mayer: 5, 13, 21, 95, 120, 147, 158
Jesse Karnes: 34, 52, 59, 90, 110
Mollie VanDerBos: 111, 113, 156
Darius Dixon: 117, 150
Alice Wright: 15
Beth Pepper: 157 (bottom)

TABLE OF CONTENTS

– Introduction –

Life Is Not a Dress Rehearsal

You only get one chance at life. Who's writing your life story?

Do you know where you're going and why? When you come to forks in the road, do you choose your path deliberately or just coast along in the deepest ruts? Are you enjoying the adventure of your life journey or finding it an arduous trek?

Do you have the courage to get off autopilot and to take responsibility for directing your life and writing your own story? If you pick up this book, you are committing to taking charge of your life. You are ready to give up the excuses, to stop blaming others, and to put in real effort—because only *you* can find *your* answers.

Do you feel trapped like a hamster in a wheel, running hard but getting nowhere? Things will not change unless you step off. If you find yourself repeating the same mistakes—in any arena of your life—then you are overdue for serious self-reflection. Life is not a dress rehearsal. The time to make your days meaningful and satisfying is right now.

Passport 2 Purpose is about stepping off the treadmill to nowhere to regroup, to analyze the path of your past, and to replot your journey with real direction and purpose. We are here to help.

Where are you going in life?

That is the central question behind this book. It is a platform for self-exploration. Throughout each chapter, there are Journal Entry pages, where you may personalize the exploration by reflecting upon yourself and your life. We highly recommend that you take time for these meditations, although you certainly need not use all of them. Pay attention, though, when one catches your eye, as that likely indicates an unresolved issue for you. This is not an assignment on which you will be graded! It is a gift to yourself.

Have you lost your way?

Many of us feel lost. The teen confused about who and what she might become, the college student who discovered he chose the wrong major, the young adult who got her dream job and found she hates it, the newly unemployed, those with so many interests and so much potential they don't know how to focus on one, those who have retired and have the luxury of time to do what they want, those who have suffered losses that upend their lives—all have in common that "*Now, what?*" sense of being lost without a guide.

We are offering you a guide, a map, a compass, a passport to a future filled with purpose and satisfaction. We cannot tell you what you should do, of course, but we have successfully led others through the process of figuring it out for themselves.

Where you should go depends entirely upon who you are. Yet few of us spend much time or get much help in analyzing ourselves. We are certain that making the effort to know yourself is time that could not be better spent. The alternative is drifting aimlessly through life, rather than setting off on a journey with a clear idea of where you are going and why.

Getting to know yourself means deciding what you value and believe.

Who are you, really?

Who do you want to become?

What are your beliefs and values?

Do your actions line up with your beliefs?

Do you have a sense of purpose for your life?

How are you making a difference in the lives of others?

We guide you through determining your personal answers to these important questions.

Does the way you live truly reflect what you say you value and believe?

Once we can say definitively what we stand for, do we prove it with our actions? Much of the unhappiness and dysfunction in our lives can be traced back to a disconnect between our values and our behavior. We can help you understand why that is so.

Have you thought deeply about how your childhood experiences have molded your feelings and reactions as an adult? Are you unconsciously replaying childhood roles without questioning why? Are you driven to act in ways that are not in your own best interests? Insight into your own history can allow you to live more intentionally, to assert the control that is rightfully yours.

No one is an island.

We may think that we come into this world alone and we leave this world alone but, for most of our days here, we are in casual or significant relationships with others. We believe that no one can be truly happy as a loner, since we are innately social creatures, but we often need help negotiating this tricky terrain. There is an inherent tension between asserting our individuality and modifying our behavior to allow for the reciprocal give-and-take of successful relationships.

A deep understanding of who you are, at your core, and how you want to live will guide you in building and preserving rewarding relationships throughout life. Only when you understand your unconscious impulses and their sources can you choose to override them. Only when you know exactly who you are looking for can you choose complementary souls for the voluntary relationships that bring you joy. Developing wisdom about what life has taught you will give you the tools needed to repair relationships that have become disappointing or unfulfilling.

That is why there is a "2" in our title: as difficult as they can be, relationships are the source of our most enduring life satisfaction. How crucial it is to be in relationship with others that we strive to be like, with whom we accomplish tasks that are important to us, who can support and advise us when the journey is bumpy or even outright catastrophic.

With the right direction and companions, the pleasure and satisfaction of your journey may surprise you.

- Journey 1 -

Beliefs & Values

Your life should stand for something. Does it? Do you stand on a strong foundation? Do you have a moral compass that steers you on your life journey? When people say one thing but do another, we call them two-faced or hypocritical. When they do as they say, we consider them genuine and authentic. Which are you?

Defining the beliefs that define you

Beliefs express our individual theories about how people and the world work. They are developed through our experiences over time and therefore vary from person to person. These core beliefs determine what we value—what we think is important and worthwhile. And these beliefs and values essentially dictate our behavior. They make us who we are.

Your beliefs and values will not necessarily agree with those of the authors. We will obviously reveal ours, because we could not write this book otherwise. We are not asserting that they are the only ones or the right ones to hold. Rather, we believe that every individual should and must discover, develop, and live by his or her own beliefs and values—that this is the secret to a life lived well.

When we say that someone has integrity, we mean that their actions align with their values. They do not experience the dissonance and discomfort of saying one thing and doing another. Instead, their lives are relatively harmonious and much less troubled by guilt or regret. They have no more ultimate control over what happens to them than anyone else, but they handle the things that are under their control well. This allows them more peace and satisfaction than those who only "talk the talk."

There is a reason why living with integrity is not more common: most people do not actually know what they believe and value.

The very first journey on the path to a more satisfying and purposeful life must be an exploration inward to discover exactly what you believe about life, human behavior, and the way the world works. In fact, our actions usually *do* demonstrate our beliefs and values—just not the ones we consciously *think* we hold.

This is because our brains work on two tracks, the conscious and the unconscious. We are under the impression that our conscious mind is like a conductor orchestrating our lives. In reality, though, the unconscious mind is in charge. It is the source of all our instinctive reactions. Whenever we "act without thinking," it is calling the shots.

Uncovering your secret world view

It is almost as if we are two people in one: the powerful secret partner who makes things happen and the fast talker who tries to explain those actions after the fact. The premise of this book is that the fast-talking conscious mind can—with deep introspection—uncover secret beliefs and values, understand their origins, and actually choose to change them. But they can only be changed after you have discovered what they are.

Just as babies construct theories about physical laws through experience—comprehending gravity through repeatedly dropping things, for example—they also build elaborate models of what they can expect from human behavior. This world view will often remain taken for granted and below the level of conscious awareness, just like our assumptions about the physical world. We have another set of more conscious beliefs that we can easily express in words, but these may be unrelated to the core beliefs on the basis of which we instinctively behave.

The task before you, and the point of this book, is to align both sets of beliefs and values. You should never be "of two minds" about such important things. Most of us struggle to articulate our beliefs and values, yet these should form the bedrock upon which we build our lives. They are both our foundation and our compass for navigating through life while remaining true to ourselves.

No one can identify your beliefs and values but you!

There is no cookbook or shortcut to defining who you are and want to become; it takes time and effort. Begin by noting how you act every day, because your actions reveal your personal values. Are you rude to clerks and cashiers because you think them unworthy of your consideration? Are you kind to strangers in need because you believe a cooperative society is a stronger one? Do you sabotage relationships because you assume people will abandon you or let you down? Does your manner and tone of voice at home show that you care about family members' concerns? Do you treat others with disdain because you believe you are much smarter or more important? Beliefs underlie what we choose to say to and do around others throughout the day. Beliefs are reflected in the attitudes we display toward them. These beliefs and attitudes are *choices*.

Others subconsciously pick up on the attitudes we express, the behaviors we exhibit, and how we handle difficult situations and people. Our actions embody our beliefs. Everyone sees who we really are and what beliefs we stand on by noting our words and actions.

Do you find that you act like a different person when among different groups of people? The people we choose as friends will significantly influence our beliefs, values, character, and life choices, whether they intend to or not. We had best choose our associates carefully.

Finding our way

When we do not know and live by our beliefs and values, it seems as if we are living in a wilderness. We easily get lost. We may lose hope and a sense of purpose. We often make poor choices about relationships, finances, studies, careers, and use of any free time. We are too impulsive or too easily led astray by companions. We may feel like a rat trying to find his way through a complicated maze. It can seem as if we are going nowhere at all, either running in circles or just stalled out, like a sailboat becalmed on a windless day.

The key to having purpose and direction in our lives lies in taking the time to define our core beliefs and values and who we hope to become. The first step is to set aside time in our days to be alone with ourselves. Our advice is to keep this journal and write in it daily. We'll provide some ideas for what you might reflect on and write about. Find a quiet and peaceful place where you won't be interrupted or distracted. Resist the temptation to give the "right" answer. Truly reflect on where you are and why. Writing your responses from the heart will help you see your growth when you review these entries later.

JOURNAL ENTRY 1

Do you enjoy being alone? Why or why not?

_____

_____

_____

_____

_____

_____

_____

_____

_____

ENTRY 2

Do you run away from being with yourself? How do you escape from being alone with your thoughts?

Are you always busy, chronically over-scheduled? Do you eat standing up or in the car? Are you always on call? Is music or a television always on at home? Must you always be in a relationship? Do you resist thinking about things?

What are your everyday tricks for avoiding introspection?

_____

_____

_____

_____

_____

_____

_____

_____

Why we need to be alone with our thoughts

We need "down" time to process our experiences. Research has proven—and you probably know from experience—that revisiting a topic several times results in lasting learning, whereas "cramming" knowledge only lasts a few days. This is likely because the repetitive stimulus prompts the growth of new nerve cells to make specific connections within our brains. These axons snake their way through our system to make literally direct connections (even as long as a single cell stretching between our toes and the base of our spines). More experience produces more and more complex connections. That is how we consolidate our learning, and that is what allows us to synthesize new ideas through combination. There is plenty of experimental and anecdotal evidence that unconscious processing goes on nearly all the time (even in our dreams, some believe). That is why you can recall that elusive name or solve that puzzle *after* you stop thinking about it consciously—it "pops into your head" from your hard-at-work unconscious mind.

We believe that we should be devoting time to *conscious* processing of our experiences, as well, since that is how we can override our unconscious verdicts, feelings, and impulses. For example, writing an annual report or preparing for a performance review forces us to revisit all we have accomplished since the last one. In the rush of daily deadlines, we can come to believe that we never finish anything, that nothing is ever done as well as we'd like, and that many projects were complete failures. Looking back with an analytical eye, though, we usually see just how much we have achieved. Those failures were the occasion for significant learning and often had side benefits we had not considered. Our unconscious impression of inefficiency and ineffectiveness is replaced with a new belief in our own competence and productivity. Looking back was a valuable use of our time.

Deliberately rethinking and re-evaluating the past experiences that have formed our emotional belief system can be similarly enlightening. We can see things from a new perspective, even when we still think the experiences were painful. That is why older people truly believe that "This, too, shall pass" and "What doesn't kill you makes you stronger." They have been through trauma more than once and fully realize it is survivable. They are much less likely to be suicidal than young people for this very reason. They *know* the world has not come to an end.

Introspection and reflection are how we make sense of and learn from our experiences. Without that effort, we continue to react on instinct alone. Reprocessing your past can give you the same gift of perspective. That is why these journaling exercises are so important and profoundly meaningful. No one else can rewrite your story but you.

ENTRY 3

Do you like the person you are? __ *Yes* __ *No* __ *Sometimes*

Why? Does something you said or did trouble you or make you proud? Write it down. What do you think this behavior said about who you are?

_____

_____

_____

_____

_____

_____

_____

_____

_____

_____

_____

_____

_____

_____

_____

_____

_____

_____

ENTRY 4

Can you recall a time when you thought your life was over? What had happened to make you believe this? What has happened since to prove that your belief was wrong?

_____

_____

_____

_____

_____

_____

_____

_____

_____

_____

_____

_____

_____

_____

_____

_____

_____

Personal Beliefs Revealed

Beliefs and values are the foundation that allows you to be your authentic self. When you meet someone, interview for a job, or interact with family and friends, are you being the "real you"? Can you express who you are? Do you know what guides you in making choices about your thoughts, words, and actions?

When you know your personal beliefs and values, you are essentially the same person 24 hours a day and 365 days a year. This does not mean that you do not play different roles, moderating speech, dress, and behavior to be appropriate to the setting. But you don't cave in to peer pressure to be, say, or do something that doesn't line up with your beliefs and values. You are "comfortable in your own skin." You don't morph into being what others want you to be. You don't wake up after an experience with remorse, regret, guilt, or shame. You aren't nervous when interrupted at work, since you don't do personal banking, shopping, or emailing when you should be working. When chatting with a friend or family member, you don't become embarrassed or quickly and awkwardly try to change the subject when someone else enters the room. You have no worry or concern if an email or text message accidentally becomes public. If someone asks others about you, he gets a similar story about your character. From friends, family, and colleagues, the same story of who you are, what you do, and how you act surfaces.

That is the key about beliefs and values — they set the parameters of our lives. They shape what we do, what we think, whom we befriend, whom we help, whom we turn to, where we work and volunteer, and what we say. They mold our hopes, dreams, causes, and passions. They influence our career choices. They impact our families and friendships. They affect the volunteer work we engage in and the charities we support with time and money. In diverse and important ways, they define who we are.

ENTRY 5

How would you describe your principles, values, or "code of conduct" to a stranger, friend, or family member? Give specific examples of how your behavior lives out these values — or of when you fall short of your ideal.

_____

_____

_____

_____

_____

_____

_____

_____

_____

_____

_____

_____

_____

_____

_____

_____

_____

_____

Time for a change?

Contemplate this life principle: ***Our actions always follow our beliefs.*** Our behavior is a manifestation of what we truly believe and value — not of what we say we do. Once you begin reflecting upon your behavior and probing for the values hidden beneath, you may not like what you find. If so, there is no better time to make some changes.

For example, we may think we believe that "family is important." Many of us betray this standard by always putting work first. We miss important family events, even when we promised to be there, to cope with unexpected work demands. We are never really "off the clock," but always on call via phone and email. We rarely give undivided attention to family members, as our thoughts are always elsewhere. Our actions do not match this professed belief. Our true belief appears to be that work is our first priority and more important than family.

Or, we may assert that all humans have inherent dignity and deserve to be treated with respect. Yet we find upon observation that we treat others thoughtlessly when they cannot do anything for us or to us. We take for granted everything that family members do for us but are quick to criticize when they don't do something. On our report card or job review, our teacher or boss notes that we talk in class or consult a cell phone in meetings. We are often late. We look down on others who are different and show it in our faces and language. The evidence shows that, actually, we believe we are superior, that our inferiors deserve less than we do, and that others exist to serve our needs.

Or, we may think that we value kindness. (Some studies say that is the trait most sought, by both men and women, in a life partner.) Unfortunately, we often discount this quality in both ourselves and others. We may react to an act of kindness as if it were a sign of weakness and then take advantage of the other person. We may blame the poor, the sick, and the unemployed for their predicaments and begrudge them assistance that costs us anything. We may make unkind assumptions about the motives of others and excoriate them for what we *think* they meant or did. Perhaps we are routinely curt with both strangers and loved ones, because we are too busy to cater to their need for attention. Obviously, we really believe that people get what they deserve, that only the strong survive, that we are too important to waste effort on being nice unless there is something immediately in it for us.

These are the kinds of painful insights that can motivate us to change. If we don't like who we are, we can do something about it! Although we probably don't consistently behave in ways that shame or disappoint us, we all do at times.

Now think about behavior that you are proud to own.

Perhaps you support a friend in things that don't interest you, just for the sake of the friendship. You mow lawns or clear snow for elderly neighbors. Maybe you volunteer when there is nothing in it for you except support for a cause. Or you recall times when you have made yourself a target in order to stand up for someone who was being bullied or abused in some way. You were honest when no one was looking, returning that lost money or refraining from cheating when it would have been easy to do so. You set aside your concerns to devote your full attention to a child who needed it. You took your obligation to serve on a jury seriously, not trying to get out of it even though it was inconvenient. You lost sleep to fly to the side of a friend in need. You held your tongue when you really wanted to lash out. There are many ways in which our behavior demonstrates beliefs and values that we are glad to acknowledge.

Since beliefs and values are the source and director of behavior, we should deliberately and consciously choose ours, rather than simply absorbing them subconsciously. And choosing them alone will not be enough to change our behavior. Since we acquired our unconscious beliefs and values over a lifetime of experiences, it will take time and practice to develop new habits to the point where they become as automatic as our old reactions. At first, we will find ourselves sliding back into old habit patterns, driven by old values that we no longer subscribe to. We will have to regularly check our behavior for evidence of the hidden drivers beneath but, eventually, action becomes belief. Once we have internalized our chosen values—made them as instinctive as the old discarded values once were—it will be much easier to live them.

ENTRY 6

Do you know the kind of person you want to become? Describe this ideal. How would you behave in a variety of circumstances?

_____

_____

_____

_____

_____

_____

_____

_____

_____

_____

_____

_____

_____

_____

_____

_____

_____

_____

ENTRY 7

Choose one of the following relationship categories to write about: your spouse or significant other; your closest friends; your coworkers or other colleagues; or someone you follow in the news, entertainment, athletic, spiritual, academic, or career world.

What were your actions, words, or thoughts today or this week related to this person or group?

Looking at them, what underlying beliefs and values do they reveal?

What do you like and not like about this behavior? What changes do you want to make?

_____

_____

_____

_____

_____

_____

_____

_____

_____

_____

_____

_____

_____

_____

_____

_____

_____

_____

_____

ENTRY 8

What beliefs do you want to have? Choose one and write it down. Underneath, write down specific actions, thoughts, or words that would be "proof" of this belief. For example:

Belief: *I believe I can become more than I am today.*

ACTIONS:

I am committed to reading widely and often, because I value learning; I belong to a public library and am willing to spend my money on books.

I am open to trying and learning new things. I go to new places, ask people to teach me their special skill, and listen to those unlike me with an open mind.

I deliberately expose myself to many viewpoints — through a variety of websites, television programs, newspapers, magazines, and books. I make time for stimulating conversation.

I regularly push myself to do and learn and read things that are difficult for me, because I won't grow unless challenged.

Your Chosen Belief:

_____

_____

ACTIONS:

Learning from a Child

It can seem like an insurmountable task to dredge up and change the beliefs and values we have absorbed over a lifetime. They are such a deeply buried, unquestioned part us that we wonder whether it is even possible. We'd like to share a story of someone who did manage to live without a disconnect between conscious and unconscious mind, whose behavior aligned well with what he *said* he believed and with his true beliefs.

We used to offer a "Beliefs and Values" workshop for college-aged mentors, middle school mentees, and their parents and grandparents. We introduced ourselves by stating our names and sharing someone we really looked up to and one reason why. The facilitator translated what was shared into a chart of "What Beliefs Special People in Our Lives Hold."

Then we asked participants to say aloud a few of their own beliefs and values. The mentors and adults were speechless and a few even appeared a little bored. Seventh grader Mario stood up and firmly stated, as he glanced around the circle of people, "Don't you have anything or anyone that you would go down on the sword for? I do."

This twelve-year-old was wise beyond his years. No doubt he was greatly influenced by his parents, grandparents, youth pastor, siblings, cousins, teachers, coaches, and friends. When asked about who and what experiences had really impacted him so far in his life, Mario had lots of stories to share. Some made you want to cry; other stories made you chuckle or laugh. As three years passed in this middle school mentoring program, many adults (and certainly Mario's peers) grew because of our relationship with him. We learned from him as he openly shared how he approached daily living with all the roller coaster rides of emotions and choices that naturally occur for a young teen. Mario was very transparent about expressing what he was grappling with in a wide range of choices and situations at school, on teams, in his home, at his church, with friends, and in his broader neighborhood and community.

From an adult's vantage point, Mario's life was far from easy. The heartache, loss, roadblocks, bullying, and obstacles this child and his family had faced were simply incredible. He seemed to know intuitively that hard times can break you down or help you grow in character. Certainly, he knew that tough times tested one's beliefs and values—he told us so!

As adults stumbled on how to answer the questions "What do you believe in?" and "What are your personal values?" our Mario would calmly and boldly state his and provide without any prompting some life examples. For anyone who listened to him over those three years and in many workshops, this child was an extraordinary mentor and teacher in our midst.

The heavy influence of life companions was reflected by both values Mario adopted from them and those he rejected. As an immigrant, he had been prompted to think often about cultural differences. He had developed clear ideas of the man he intended to become. This is precisely the kind of analysis and planning we all should be doing. And we must all become more aware of how the beliefs, values, and behavior of our companions affect our own.

How important it is to regularly spend time with people who know who they are and what they stand for. They are gifts. They can truly shape who we are and who we become. Often, the best teachers are our children and teens. Mario certainly impacted dozens of children and adults during those precious years together. One can only assume that he continues to influence others today as a young man.

If you are having difficulty making changes in your life, think about changing your companions. Let those you admire and want to emulate influence you more frequently and directly.

ENTRY 9

Who are the children and teens in your life now? What beliefs do you think they have? What actions provide evidence that they have those beliefs?

How do they treat themselves, you, and others? What do they say about themselves, you, and others?

If you admire the values their behavior reveals, how can you tell them so?

_____

_____

_____

_____

_____

_____

_____

_____

_____

_____

_____

ENTRY 10

For good or ill, we are role models for the young people in our lives. They notice and emulate what we do much more than what we say. For example:

Belief: *I believe in living within (or below) my means.*

ACTIONS:

I buy things I can pay for now. I have a budget and stick to it, avoiding impulse buys. I think twice before I buy clothes, shoes, or tickets to a movie. Often I don't need things, or I can rent a movie on DVD. I make my own coffee, breakfasts, and lunches instead of buying them.

I don't always get "the best" of everything or indulge myself in luxuries "because I'm worth it." I know that "good enough" is often plenty, and that wants are not the same thing as needs.

I take my paycheck and save some, give some to others, pay bills, and buy something (even if it's from the Dollar Store) for me.

How do you talk and act around children and teens? What underlying beliefs are you witnessing to them by how you behave with or around them? Pick one belief you can model through actions.

Belief:

_____

_____

ACTIONS:

_____

_____

_____

_____

_____

_____

_____

_____

_____

_____

_____

Origins of Beliefs & Values

It is the authors' belief that humans are inherently social and do nothing in isolation. We are the products of our lifetime of relationships and experiences. It has taken us all of our lives to get to this moment, and our unconscious value system sums up everything we think we know about the world.

We begin building that mental model in our earliest relationship, usually with our mothers. Our estimation of what we can expect from others is most strongly influenced by our early caregivers. We are born helpless, completely dependent upon others to figure out and fill our needs. Those caregivers need not be experts for us to do well, for babies are quite resilient, but they do have to be responsive if we are to thrive.

When others let us down

If, as infants, we go for long periods hungry, wet, and cold, we learn to perceive the world as a harsh and painful place. If we are abused in childhood, we may come to believe we are bad—for the child's sense of causality can be primitive and wrong. Children commonly feel at fault for things they did not cause and could not have prevented. If we grow up with unpredictable violence, we may become either timid or aggressive—fearing what we don't understand or imitating it. Most child abusers were, themselves, victims of abuse. They have

internalized the idea that this behavior is normal.

If we are ignored or in some way abandoned as children (even via death—children may interpret any leaving as intentional), we may find it very difficult to trust others or to express affection. Unconsciously, we believe that everyone we love eventually leaves, so why take the chance of getting attached to anyone? If we see small signs of restiveness in a relationship, somewhere deep inside we believe the end is near—so we may bring things to a head with a fight, or walk out before we can be deserted … again.

If important adults let us down in childhood, we learn to believe that no one can be relied upon. Our mental model tells us that we all sink or swim on our own. As a consequence, we tend to be less empathetic and available to others. Experience taught us to believe that it's a dog-eat-dog world, that you have to look out for Number One. We will be unlikely, therefore, to value cooperation or charity. We may be ruthlessly competitive. We'll tend to put ourselves first always. At some deep level, we believe that our personal prerogatives take precedence over our social obligations.

When others come through for us

Just as inadequate early relationships can set you up for a lifetime of disappointment, responsive ones can give you the security and confidence to expect good things in life.

A baby who is loved and cared for, even imperfectly (as surely all of us are), assumes that he always will be—and that he is worthy of love and care. If we are helped when in trouble and tended when sick, we believe that everyone deserves the same. If we experienced a warm and supportive family in childhood, that is our model for the family we establish in adulthood. If someone sacrificed selflessly to meet our needs, we believe that is how we should behave later. If our autonomy and opinions are respected, we believe that everyone's should be.

If we have experienced and therefore believe in the interdependence of relationships, then we will value the kindness, compassion, and generosity that we know enable us to be more together than we are separately.

Usually, we are unaware of the assumptions we make because of our childhood experiences. For example, one of the authors came from a large and happy family. When her father asked her and her siblings to share their strong childhood memories for his autobiography, he was dismayed that most such memories were of the few times he had lost his temper or otherwise behaved poorly. The reason those memories stood out was that they were anomalies. They had regularly enjoyed fun times together. Picnics, trips to the beach, forays to enjoy fireworks, and family reunions were routine events. The entire family would turn out every light in the house to play Hide and Go Seek. Daily family dinners were the occasion to draw each of them out in conversation. These things were not mentioned because they were like the water in a fishbowl—completely taken for granted by the fish. The siblings grew up thinking that every family was like theirs, and that all siblings grew to adulthood as fast friends. To this day, this writer is naïve about others with hidden or ulterior motives, because it does not occur to her that people can be devious and manipulative. She learned early and well to trust and count on others.

If we experience good things repeatedly, we come to expect them. We believe they will and should continue to happen, and we put a high value on them. We call these "formative experiences" because they mold us into who we become.

ENTRY 11

What was your own early childhood like? What warm and supportive memories come to mind? What chaotic, insecure, or deeply traumatic memories arise?

_____

_____

_____

_____

_____

_____

_____

_____

_____

_____

_____

_____

_____

_____

_____

_____

_____

_____

_____

_____

ENTRY 12

How have your most memorable childhood experiences affected your view of yourself? An unexpected death can make you feel insecure and unworthy, worried that a loved one may leave you at any time. A sympathetic adult focusing on you alone can make you feel loved and worthy—something you still believe decades later. If you dropped the ball that lost the crucial game, did you internalize the belief that you just don't have what it takes? What do your strongest memories say about your self-concept?

_____

_____

_____

_____

_____

_____

_____

_____

_____

_____

_____

_____

_____

_____

_____

_____

_____

_____

ENTRY 13

The most memorable experiences from your childhood have also shaped your unconscious beliefs about others. What have you come to expect from family holiday dinners, weddings, graduations, funerals, reunions? How do you expect friends, colleagues, and even strangers to behave? What's the story behind your expectations? Are you still holding a child's perspective on long-ago events? How can you rewrite or edit the story to allow you to change your beliefs?

_____

_____

_____

_____

_____

_____

_____

_____

_____

_____

_____

_____

_____

_____

What if we missed out in childhood?

This theory—of mental models shaped by experience that unconsciously dictate our adult behavior—seems too deterministic, and it is. Although propelled by our hidden hypotheses, we are not irreversibly controlled by them. Once we are aware of them, we can override the impulses they generate. We can decide to change our model, to rewrite our story, to form new habits that both spring from and support new beliefs and values.

There is an old experiment that suggests one deliberately set out to compliment, blatantly appreciate, and treat with kindness an intimate partner when the relationship has grown stale and unsatisfying. It can feel inauthentic to act in a way that is no longer instinctive, but research appears to confirm that this fake-it-'til-you-make-it technique can actually work. Repeated behavior wears a new groove in our habit patterns, we begin to really feel what we go through the motions of feeling, and our behavior is reflected back to us by our partner in a way that engenders and amplifies good feelings on both sides. That is to say, we can change how we feel and what we believe by changing our habits.

Our unconscious model was constructed by repeated experiences, but the process can work in reverse. If we give enough sustained effort to behaving in new ways, we can remodel our model. Our repeated new experiences wear new grooves, so that we feel different and make different assumptions.

Beliefs and values evolve

We can change our world view because, although very powerful, it does change over time. We are not prisoners of our childhood experiences. And our early caregivers are not the only important adults who can model for us a way to be.

Social science research indicates that a single caring adult—a teacher, coach, grandparent, mentor, older sibling, neighbor, uncle, etc.—can make all the difference in a child's life. Having just one admired person support and believe in you can be all it takes to change your mental model of how the world works and what you are capable of.

Peers, too, can have great influence — as any parent of a teenager can attest. Child bullies, teenage cliques, fraternities and sororities, high school marching bands and drama clubs, Facebook friends, sports teams, workplace groups, corporate cultures, fraternal organizations, extended families, workout buddies, political parties—all these affiliations tell us what is normal in human relationships, how to behave, what to expect, and what to value.

If we are disappointed in how we act among certain groups, we can find new groups and allow their norms and values to seep into us. This is the premise behind the famous Harlem Children's Zone, which includes much more than schools. The program also provides "baby college" for expectant parents, pre-school and after-school programs, healthy meals and in-school medical and dental care, block associations, playgrounds and parks, and renovated housing. It attempts to completely change the habits, norms, and expectations of children living in poverty by changing every aspect of their environment. They are exposed to and absorb completely new ways of thinking and doing.

Similarly, we can choose to join new groups or to stop spending free time with those whose beliefs and values we no longer share. Being around others who are simpatico reinforces the habits of thought and action that we now want to ingrain into our unconscious minds.

If changing groups is too difficult (as it may be in a job-related association), we can bring our perceptions and objections to the attention of the group and attempt to change the culture. We can be the influencer instead of the influenced. After all, why should we not take on a leadership role?

Challenge provokes growth

We believe that people are unlikely to change if they are satisfied with the status quo. It is only when our assumptions are challenged in some way that we recognize them consciously and, perhaps, rethink them. We experience some cognitive dissonance: things do not follow our internal model, our expectations are not borne out, we experience strong regret, the disconnect between our professed values and our behavior is brought to our attention. This is uncomfortable and calls for resolution.

For some people, a single Moment of Truth, when their own hypocrisy is exposed, may be enough to reform their behavior and reconstitute their values. But that is uncommon.

Think how many of us rationally accept that we eat the wrong things or drink too much alcohol or need to get more exercise, but how few of us actually follow through on these alleged beliefs. If we really believed those things, wouldn't we *do something* about them?

The reason we do not is "reason" itself. We lie to ourselves all the time about what we believe, value, and do. We are expert rationalizers and excuse-makers. Our unconscious beliefs are really running the show. Deep down, we believe we are invulnerable and immortal. Bad things will never happen to *us*. We are in a state of persistent denial. We believe we have plenty of slack—unlimited time to get ourselves together and change our habits, *later*. Even the "wonderfully concentrated mind" after a near-death experience loses focus soon enough. We haven't truly changed our beliefs.

"Interventions" for alcoholics and drug abusers recognize that being confronted with the truth is not enough to change addictive behavior. They are designed to drive someone into a treatment program. There, actual behavior is changed through both coercion and support. If new patterns can be engraved in our subconscious minds, our beliefs and subsequent behavior really can change. The alcoholic may have to avoid family and change friends, and is warned not to spend time in bars or take even one drink. Parents of an obese child support him by limiting the kinds of food available at home and by changing their own behavior. Parents who want a teen to stop smoking will make a pact to quit together, thus supporting one another in making the change. Friends or relatives who want to be more active will often do better together than if they had tried to change as individuals.

Changes in our surroundings and companions, as well as mutual support agreements, are powerful ways to help us form new habit patterns. The old patterns still linger, waiting to be reactivated by subtle encouragement. Sometimes, the best way to control our impulses is to control our environment so that they never arise.

ENTRY 14

Is there someone you spend time with who you know you are not your "best self" with? What kinds of things do you say and do when with this person that you are embarrassed by or ashamed of? Can you change your pattern of interactions? Might you be better off letting go of this relationship?

_____

_____

_____

_____

_____

_____

_____

_____

_____

_____

_____

_____

_____

_____

_____

ENTRY 15

Who is someone you believe does more than talk — someone who "walks the walk"? You know this person's beliefs because of what he or she says and does with you and with others.

Elaborate on what this person has said and done that demonstrates these beliefs.

_____

_____

_____

_____

_____

_____

_____

_____

_____

_____

_____

_____

_____

_____

Choosing New Beliefs

Now that we have been uncovering our real, unconscious beliefs, we may want to adopt new ones. We can see that the old ones have been controlling us in ways that have not worked for us — we are not satisfied with our present lives or the direction we are heading.

These unconscious drivers of our behavior have always evolved, throughout the stages of our lives. Early on, we tend to absorb the beliefs and values of our parents and family members. Teens' beliefs are influenced and challenged by peers or other adults that they look up to as role models. Experiences and relationships with people of similar or different religions also cause us to reassess our own beliefs. In healthy lifelong development, we are always becoming our own unique persons. Through this journaling and self-reflection process, we are now ready to take a more active role in choosing what we believe and deem worthwhile. But where to start?

Here are some "I believe" statements that may help you think about what foundational beliefs you want to stand on. These came from many participants in our *Michigan Reach Out* mentoring programs.

"I believe I should be a more honest and trustworthy person."

"I believe in taking care of my body."

"I believe I have the power to choose my own attitude every morning."

"I believe my life has a purpose to better the world — starting with my family and community."

"I believe people are 'givers' or 'grabbers' and that 'grabbers' can become 'givers.'"

"I believe I can make a difference in someone else's life."

"I believe family is more important than anything else."

"I believe I can create a happier family than the one I grew up in."

"I believe 'giving back' and 'serving others' are critical for life to have meaning."

"I believe you treat people the way you want to be treated—all the time."

"I believe if I invest in one other person's life, it can make an impact on the world."

"I believe that to whom much is given, much is required."

"I believe I can help to end world hunger."

"I believe in life after death."

"I believe in always telling the truth."

"I believe that people, not things or accomplishments, have been the real source of happiness in my life."

"I believe I am a work in progress and will always be growing and learning."

"I believe that what doesn't kill me makes me stronger."

"I believe I should respect others' opinions and ideas."

"I believe I can disagree with others' opinions and values without questioning their motives."

"I believe education is the key to my future."

"I believe in destiny and a loving God."

"I believe every person is precious and unique."

"I believe in forgiveness."

"I believe people's behavior will rise to meet your expectations."

ENTRY 16

Circle at least 5 statements of beliefs from the previous pages that are already yours. Write them down. How did you come to hold these convictions? Who influenced you and what experiences led you to these beliefs?

After this analysis, do you still believe these things? Should you?

_____

_____

_____

_____

_____

_____

_____

_____

_____

_____

_____

_____

_____

_____

ENTRY 17

Is there one belief that you want to focus on and further develop as your own? Write it down.

Now create an action plan for living this belief with the people and situations in your life. Note the words and actions that would show you hold this belief.

_____

_____

_____

_____

_____

_____

_____

_____

_____

_____

_____

_____

_____

_____

_____

_____

_____

_____

ENTRY 18

Looking at the person you are and the person you want to become, must changes be made in your life?

For example, do you need to make it a priority to spend time with yourself? To invest in reading, praying, meditating, reflecting, and journaling? To find a mentor to help you on your journey to develop and live out chosen beliefs? To change the people you spend time with because their beliefs just don't line up with yours? To change the people or the music to which you listen, or the television shows, movies, and websites that influence you?

What steps can you take to change the environment that shapes who you are?

_____

_____

_____

_____

Choosing New Values

Our instinctive value judgments flow from our unconscious beliefs. But sometimes it is easier to consciously decide what we value and attempt to change that. This is because hidden beliefs can actually be harder to bring into the light than hidden values. We understand the language of values immediately, even if we often deceive ourselves about what we really value, deep inside.

Values are our ideals, our judgments about what is important and worthwhile. While they vary from person to person, they are very much influenced by our families and cultures. Every environment has its own hidden "code of conduct" that tells its inhabitants how they should speak to friends and to strangers, dress for different occasions, handle conflict, defer to or challenge authority, behave when no one is looking, discipline and care for children, balance the rights of the individual with the needs of the group, and so on. We absorb values as "cultural norms"—they tell us how to be normal in that group.

**If beliefs encode how we perceive the world,
values prescribe how we interact with it.**

Values are demonstrated in how we live every day. They are reflected in what we do, whom we choose to be with, what we are trying to accomplish, who we want to become, how we spend our time, and how we treat ourselves and others. Values are often exposed during a hard time, a difficult relationship, or a crisis. We can see what we value by examining what we do with our time and our money. Values are our priorities.

Your values arose in the context of your life experience. If you now want to change these "inherited" values, it can be helpful to examine the possibilities. There are many positive and strong values to consider adopting. Here are some that can guide you on the journey to take control of your life and to steer it in directions of your conscious choice. The listing is alphabetical, not in order of importance.

Accountability   Acknowledging personal responsibility for choices, actions, words, attitudes; also, taking responsibility for the consequences of our actions, even when they were not intended.

Compassion   Sympathy for the suffering of others; a desire to help the less fortunate.

Dependability	Habit of following through on commitments made to family, friends, co-workers, groups, or even strangers.
Humility	Acceptance that none of us knows everything; openness and willingness to learn from others.
Persistence	Willingness to work hard to achieve our goals; acknowledgement that something worth having must be earned, and that no one owes us what we want.
Self-discipline	The ability to delay gratification and to control impulses. This can mean controlling our desire to use drugs or alcohol; restraining sexual impulses; abstaining from physical violence and fights; keeping in check the impulse to spend money recklessly; and refraining from acting unkindly when provoked.
Selflessness	The ability to put others first; the kind of caring that allows parents to sacrifice routinely for their children—or anyone to do so on occasion for a complete stranger.

Most of these values are pro-social. They stem from beliefs that humans are inescapably social and interdependent, that we are unable to flourish outside of relationship. If we believe that, then we will value collaboration, cooperation, reciprocity, self-control, selflessness — all principles that strengthen and support relationships.

Reflecting upon your behavior in terms of value judgments can reveal to you what you unconsciously value. A quick look about us shows that many in our society value possessions, power, fame, competition, and comfort. Many apparently do not value self-denial, generosity, competence, cooperation, or sacrifice for the common good. What does your behavior reveal about your values and priorities? Do you like what you see?

It may be time to take on a new set of values and to ponder what behavior would both ingrain and demonstrate those values.

Examine and evaluate some values for potential adoption.
Choose one or more of the following and reflect upon them.

ENTRY 19

Consider the value of **accountability**: *When do you take personal responsibility for what you think, say, and do? When do you try to shrink from taking personal responsibility? Whom do you often follow and then blame for what "we" said or* *did? Do you believe you are entitled to things, to better treatment from others, to a promotion? Do you often blame someone else for what happens in your life? Do you habitually make excuses rather than face your own responsibility?*

Describe one situation in which you want to show more responsibility and how you might do so.

_____

_____

_____

_____

_____

_____

_____

_____

_____

_____

_____

_____

_____

_____

_____

_____

_____

_____

_____

_____

_____

_____

ENTRY 20

*Consider the value of **compassion**: Do you tend to blame others who are poor or sick for not trying hard enough or for not taking good enough care of themselves? Is it hard for you to feel empathy for "difficult" people?*

Looking back, when do you wish you had made more of an effort to put yourself in someone else's shoes rather than judging them? What advantages have you enjoyed that others may not?

What actions do you or might you take in your life to "give back" to others less fortunate than you are?

_____

_____

_____

_____

_____

_____

_____

_____

_____

_____

_____

_____

_____

_____

_____

_____

_____

_____

_____

ENTRY 21

Consider the value of **dependability**: *Do you let others down when they are counting on you? Do you "over-promise"? Do you think before committing yourself, and then follow through?*

Write about one time you let someone down that you really regret now. How would your lives have been different if you had not?

Write about another time when you made a commitment that you should not have. How might you have handled this differently?

_____

_____

_____

_____

_____

_____

_____

_____

_____

_____

_____

_____

_____

_____

_____

_____

_____

_____

_____

ENTRY 22

*Consider the value of **humility**: Do you act as if you know more than anyone else? Do you make a habit of putting others down? When someone tells of an accomplishment, do you have to top it with one of your own? Have you gotten into trouble by ignoring the advice of others who really did know better? Are you truly open to the idea that you can learn from others, not just in school but at work or at home? Describe when one of these situations has occurred for you.*

_____

_____

_____

_____

_____

_____

_____

_____

_____

_____

_____

_____

_____

_____

_____

_____

_____

_____

_____

_____

ENTRY 23

*Consider the value of **persistence**: Do you give up at the first hint of difficulty or frustration? Are you acting out a belief that you will never amount to anything?*

Write about one time that you should have tried harder. You were self-defeated because you threw in the towel too soon. Did you expect to be rescued? Did you fear failure and so thought it better to withdraw? What did you miss out on?

Write about another time when you accomplished something you had originally thought was beyond your capability. Perhaps you were alone and knew you had to sink or swim on your own. Having no choice, you surprised yourself with what you were able to do. How did you feel afterward? Can you build upon that strengthened self-confidence by persisting through difficulty even when you could give up?

ENTRY 24

*Consider the value of **self-discipline**: "Do as I say, not as I do" might exemplify the lack of restraint we model today for peers, teens, and children.*

For example, do you fight with, argue with, or abuse others?

What do you believe about alcohol and street or recreational drugs?

What do you believe about sexual relations in and outside of marriage?

Do you over-indulge in "things" because you feel you deserve to have them?

Do you simply react without thinking, mirroring the bad behavior of others instead of modeling a better way?

Describe areas of your life and behavior that cry out for more self-discipline and what behavior changes that implies.

_____

_____

_____

_____

_____

_____

_____

_____

_____

_____

_____

_____

_____

_____

_____

_____

_____

ENTRY 25

*Consider the value of **selflessness**: When in your life have you put another's needs before your own? When do you now wish you had? Why? What do you need to change in your life to model caring for someone else?*

_____

_____

_____

_____

_____

_____

_____

_____

_____

_____

_____

_____

_____

_____

_____

_____

_____

_____

_____

_____

_____

_____

_____

Group Beliefs and Values

Families, churches, organizations, companies, and groups of peers and friends have corporate or shared beliefs and values. Sometimes these are statements that are clearly articulated. Often, the values and beliefs of a group of people are unspoken but clearly seen in how they act and treat one another and those outside of their group. Since changing your groups is one effective way to change your beliefs and values, you need to bring these implicit codes into the light. How else can you choose groups that will help you become the person you now want to be?

For example, the *Michigan Reach Out* nonprofit organization has a core belief statement: **"We believe every person is unique, precious, worthy, and has a destiny."** Given how incredibly diverse group members have been over the years, it is amazing that every year the entire mass of people has agreed on this statement.

The statement unites us in our mission. It bonds us in treating every single person as being very special and worth our time. It encourages each of us to listen to and respect others who think, believe, or act differently than we do. We try to honestly embrace our differences. We learn about and attempt to practice genuine "active listening" for one another. We embrace that no person is better or more worthwhile than another. We don't count numbers of people at an event or outing as a sign of success. We know that if just one person comes, what we shared was worthwhile. We spend time breaking down our belief statement and sharing what we mean individually and collectively.

Other groups and organizations may not spend as much time deliberately discussing their shared beliefs and values, but they have them! Couples have them. Groups of friends have them. Teams have them. Families have them. Faith-based and nonprofit organizations have them. Companies have them.

When you don't know your personal and individual beliefs and values, you can be swayed to take on those of the workplaces, organizations, and groups you choose to be part of. That's why we emphasize the importance of **knowing who you are**. Then you can choose people and groups with whom you want to work, associate, learn, play, and spend your life!

High school athletes often choose the college to attend because of who the coach is and what they learn from making a campus visit and spending time with players. A person joining a fraternity, sorority, church, volunteer organization, or professional group will pick "the one" based on the mission and vibes they get from meeting people who are already members. Parents will select schools and even teachers based on what they see written about missions, goals, and values. A person often joins a company based on the corporate mission and goals, as well as whom they meet during interviews. Consciously or unconsciously, we are evaluating others' character, motives, beliefs, values. We are choosing to be associated with other people or groups —or to walk away.

ENTRY 26

What are your family's core beliefs and values? Have some been handed down from one generation to another? Can you ask grandparents, aunts and uncles, parents, and children what they think the family's core beliefs and values are? You can always look at the actions of elders, parents, siblings, and children to determine their beliefs and values. Write them down.

Are you starting your own family? What beliefs and values do you want to articulate and live out with your spouse and children?

Do you want your existing family to discuss and adopt new values? It won't happen unless you make it happen. How would you initiate such discussions? Write yourself a script.

_____

_____

_____

_____

_____

_____

_____

_____

_____

_____

_____

_____

_____

_____

_____

_____

ENTRY 27

Research and write down the mission, goals, principles, or values of your school, college, or employer.

Observe and think about who you see really practicing or living out these beliefs and values. Similarly, which beliefs and values are not seen in action?

Do you "fit" where you are working or going to school? Do your personal beliefs and values line up with the school's or company's? If not, how could you influence them to change?

_____

_____

_____

_____

_____

_____

_____

_____

_____

_____

_____

_____

_____

_____

_____

ENTRY 28

To what organizations or churches do you belong? Describe their mission, goals, principles, and values. Do these line up with yours?

Through what actions do leaders and members demonstrate they are seriously carrying out their beliefs and values? How can you help them?

_____

_____

_____

_____

_____

_____

_____

_____

_____

_____

_____

_____

_____

_____

_____

_____

What We Have Learned

A lifetime of experiences has laid down patterns in our minds. We have absorbed and adapted beliefs and values through repeated experiences. We may not always be aware of these patterns, since they are now automatic.

Just as an experienced driver can get from work to home "on autopilot," we no longer have to grapple with what to do and how throughout our day. We act without thinking. A practiced athlete or musician has very sophisticated physical skill sets developed through repetition. He no longer has to think about where to place his fingers or feet; he performs better but actually works at it less than when he was a beginner.

Our brains take similar shortcuts all the time with thinking skills. We recognize faces in a way computers could never hope to emulate. We grasp very complex concepts, not just by generalizing but by capturing their essence. We effortlessly recognize the "cup-ness" of a coffee mug, a crystal champagne flute, a tin cup, a beer stein, a sippy cup, a shot glass, even a novelty mug shaped like an animal — and do it in milliseconds with no conscious thought.

Our inner model of how the world works, how people can and should behave, and how we should react and interact is equally hidden from our conscious view. We have unconsciously mapped the world, and our behavior flows from the assumptions of that map. If our control of our behavior is imperfect, that is likely because we do not appreciate the underlying beliefs and values that drive it. Changing behavior without changing beliefs and values is very hard.

But changing beliefs and values is impossible unless we first bring them to conscious awareness. All our reflection and journaling has given us that awareness. Now we know why we have behaved in ways that did not serve us well. Now we know what beliefs and values we want to adopt to replace those that have failed us. We are ready to revert to the awkward and slow "thinking about everything" stage of beginners. Repeatedly considering what we are doing and why lets us set new habit patterns, eventually making new kinds of behavior automatic.

ENTRY 29

Beliefs and values are like a life compass. They help us know where we are and where we are going. When we make a wrong turn, get lost, or follow the wrong people, our compass can help us to return to our chosen path.

It can be helpful to think of beliefs and values in terms of simple character traits. Here is a list of qualities you might aspire to that embody values.

creative	hopeful	patient	tolerant
diligent	dependable	shy	orderly
kind	thorough	proactive	optimistic
loyal	cautious	gentle	grateful
flexible	enthusiastic	sincere	generous
persuasive	perseverant	virtuous	discerning
sensitive	compassionate	determined	hospitable
wise	conscientious	forgiving	cheerful
bold	self-controlled	faithful	committed
visionary	reliable	humble	unselfish

_____

_____

_____

_____

_____

Choose the ones that resonate most with you and circle them. Add other qualities that you would like to possess.

Write down, in a way that makes sense for you, how your chosen values can serve as a life compass for you.

My Beliefs & Values Compass

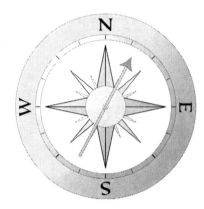

Referring to this personal compass regularly can help you to form new behavior patterns, until the values become so ingrained that you no longer have to think about how you want to behave. Your GPS will be internal.

ENTRY 30

How would you sum up and describe your life journey so far? If you were granted a couple of do-overs, what would they be and what would you do? What beliefs and values did you lack or ignore that could have prevented the behavior you now regret?

_____

_____

_____

_____

_____

_____

_____

_____

_____

_____

_____

_____

_____

_____

_____

_____

_____

_____

_____

ENTRY 31

How would you like to sum up the next chapter of your life story? What are your goals, hopes, aspirations, and dreams? What beliefs do you want others to share when they describe you?

_____

_____

_____

_____

_____

_____

_____

_____

_____

_____

_____

_____

_____

_____

_____

_____

_____

_____

Summary of Journey 1

What I say is not always what I do.

I don't actually know what I believe and value.

Uncovering my secret beliefs and values
allows me to change them.

I can be the person I really want to be.

- Journey 2 -

Healthy Boundaries

You've already done the hard work of establishing who you are. Your beliefs and values define you. This journey is all about how to protect yourself— to not lose yourself as you interact with others. Healthy boundaries between people keep our core identities intact.

We all have a basic need for relationships with others. At the same time, our ability to have healthy relationships depends a great deal on our being free to "own" and to "be" our unique selves. If we do not "own" our lives, we leave ourselves open to being controlled, persuaded, and manipulated by others. Some may want us to be like them or to live out the dreams they could not; others may insist that we live up to their ideals for a partner, mate, child, or friend.

We should have a basic conceptual framework for boundaries. They rest on the foundation of our beliefs and values and serve as a sort of life manual. We can check back to see what we have read about and written down for our personal beliefs and values. Next to every belief and value statement we examine, we should be erecting, defining, communicating, and defending appropriate boundaries. They are necessary for us to honor and protect our beliefs and values. Meanwhile, we can be more aware of and open to respecting others' beliefs and values and their boundaries. If we don't do this introspection for ourselves, we are really incapable of being true to ourselves or being respectful of others.

If we have boundaries for who we are, we have choices. We are able to set limits on the intrusion, help, advice, influence, or requests of others. Healthy boundaries directly relate to our self-image, self-confidence, self-control, and self-respect. Boundaries give us the freedom and limitless options to be ourselves. It is as if we have a fence around ourselves with many gates, allowing people to come into our space and lives appropriately and positively. These gates

allow us to decide who we give permission to share our life, learning, work, and varying experiences. When we open our gates to let others in, we can define and communicate the circumstances or parameters under which they are invited into our lives.

The individual-versus-society dilemma

The authors stand on a belief that "every person is unique, precious, worthy, and has a destiny." That simple belief statement insists that we all deserve to be our own true selves, to follow *our* dreams and passions, to have and act on causes, to realize and use our skills in meaningful careers. It requires that boundaries are communicated and honored to allow that independence. No one has the right to infringe upon our individual prerogative to chart our own life course.

There is an inherent, unavoidable tension between our rights as individuals and our obligations to others, for humans cannot live fully and happily as hermits. We need one another from the moment of conception to our death beds. Choices on where to draw the line between our personal needs and our social obligations will always be with us. No hard-and-fast rule can save us from agonizing over these decisions.

Will we be the ultimate individualists who prize personal freedom above human interdependence? Will we be doormats who let others walk all over us? Or will we constantly and carefully walk the line between these two extremes, preserving our core selves while enjoying the mutual support of healthy relationships?

Building on stone rather than sand

Most people never give a thought to who they are and what they stand for. They go through life reacting to people and events but never have the guidance of a clear purpose and defined boundaries. Now that you have built a strong foundation of values and beliefs, you can erect boundary walls that will not crack or waver when an ill wind blows. Healthy boundaries give you the freedom to be yourself, rather than a hypocrite or a people-pleaser who is driven by the needs, desires, and values of others.

Just as no one else can prescribe your personal beliefs and values, *only you* can negotiate the boundaries that arise from those you choose. The general principles and specific examples that follow may not align with your value system. They are presented to stimulate your analysis of how you want to establish boundaries that suit who *you* are.

We will learn about ways to derive boundaries from your own values and beliefs, how to communicate them to others, warning signs of intrusion into what should be your personal space, and ways to defend yourself. When we understand boundaries and establish ours on the foundation of our beliefs and values, we are able to choose people with whom we can have healthy and often life-long relationships. We are the pilots and navigators of our own life journey. We make good decisions about where we are going, with whom we are going, and what we are going to do.

How beliefs become boundaries

Beliefs—whether obvious or unstated—are key starting points for defining the limits and boundaries for each person or group. For example, families or organizations are often known for their beliefs related to such values as respect for others, openness to new ideas, creativity, persistence in the face of adversity, or loyalty. Such a reputation encourages each person in the group to uphold those shared beliefs and to act upon those values.

Ponder what your own reputation is among different people and groups with whom you associate. Think about the times you have investigated the reputation, beliefs, values, and boundaries of a school, company, or organization before you decided to join them or to work with them. Personal and group boundaries are there if we look for them. Finding the right match first requires that we know our personal beliefs, values, and boundaries. Then we are able to recognize where we will genuinely fit in and be happy.

ENTRY 32

We cannot define proper boundaries without reference to the beliefs and values from which they should stem. Look back at your Beliefs & Values Compass (on page 54). Choose one or two of the belief/value words that you adopted there and give examples of how boundaries and boundary issues might flow from them.

- *For example, people who aspire to leadership roles might value being "bold" or "visionary." Adopting that role might affect other values, such as the importance of family or personal time. Being an inspiring leader can take over your life, leaving little time to spend on family, leisure, or personal pursuits. Bold leaders may over-commit their organizations, trampling on the rights and free time of their colleagues.*

- *Someone who prizes "dependability" can easily come up with guidelines from that ideal: doing what they said they would, showing up on time, coming through when others count on them. But we may allow our lives to get out of balance if we are determined to be dependable but we can't say "no." We may commit to too many projects and end up neglecting ourselves and our families, feeling constantly guilty and inadequate, and guaranteeing a life of stress and unhappiness.*

What values do you prize? How might you pursue those ideals while maintaining the balance fostered by healthy boundaries?

_____

_____

_____

_____

_____

_____

_____

_____

_____

_____

_____

_____

_____

_____

_____

_____

_____

_____

_____

_____

_____

_____

_____

_____

_____

ENTRY 33

Can you think of a time when you were too malleable, so eager to please someone else that you compromised yourself in some way? What was the situation? Why did you feel bad or uncomfortable about your behavior? Why do you think you were unable to stand up for yourself? How might you have responded differently to such pressure?

_____

_____

_____

_____

_____

_____

_____

_____

_____

_____

_____

_____

_____

_____

_____

_____

_____

_____

_____

_____

_____

Concept of Physical Boundaries

Let us explore the general concept of boundaries. They are most easily seen as borders separating an inside and an outside. In a purely physical sense, we see them in walls, fences, and borders. Early humans created picket fences or "pales" around their villages; someone who was foreign and dangerous was "beyond the pale." They progressed to castle walls, moats, harbor fortifications, even the Great Wall of China. Such barriers imply safety within and danger without. They also necessarily involve inclusion and exclusion: only some people are allowed in, only some of the time.

Most boundaries in our lives are like these: they exist to offer us safety and freedom within them. A baby may be placed within a play pen or other enclosure. This allows freedom to play and explore within safe limits. Children may graduate to similar freedom within a fenced yard. Later, they are allowed to roam as long as they cross no streets, or as long as they are home by dark.

Adults commonly agree to similar boundary restrictions. We respect the privacy within closed doors; we knock and wait for admittance. We know that staring through windows like a Peeping Tom is just not done. We wait our turn on the road, proceeding through busy intersections only when the light turns green or the "Walk" sign is lit. At home, at school, at work, or at the gym, we respect that we have personal rooms, desks, closets, or lockers. We honor "No trespassing" signs or stay on the prepared paths or sidewalks rather than taking short cuts. We survey land and use fences or hedges to establish borders between properties. We go through Customs when crossing international borders.

All these physical boundaries contribute to a comfortable and orderly society that spells out expectations and minimizes confrontations. Once we know and obey the unwritten rules, we are all safer and happier.

ENTRY 34

What are some physical boundaries I see where I live? Do I have my own space? Do others respect my space?

What are shared spaces where I live? How do the people I live with honor and take care of that shared space?

_____

_____

_____

_____

_____

_____

_____

_____

_____

_____

_____

ENTRY 35

What are the physical boundaries I encounter during a typical day? Are there general rules that guide how people honor and respect physical boundaries in public, on the roads, at school, at work, or at the gym?

_____

_____

_____

_____

_____

_____

_____

_____

_____

ENTRY 36

Are there some physical boundaries for myself or with others that I do not respect and honor in my life at home, at school, at work, on the road, in the park, at the mall or grocery store? Why not? What kinds of problems could this cause?

_____

_____

_____

_____

_____

_____

_____

_____

_____

_____

Boundaries may require defense

One thing all boundaries have in common is that they will, either occasionally or often, require us to defend them. It seems simple to note that excluded people may want to get in. We naturally rally to defend ourselves against those who would hurt us or take something that is important to us. Children fight to protect their toys. Siblings protect one another from neighborhood bullies. Families may stand up for members against outsiders even when those being defended are in the wrong. Gangs guard their turf. Police forces ensure that people within our borders obey the rules that keep us all safe. Cities or states fight with one another over scarce resources. Societies defend their borders, with force of arms if necessary.

In these cases, it is relatively simple to see who is an insider and who the boundary is meant to exclude. Those who belong to a group, live within its borders, and follow its rules are insiders. Outsiders may be seen as the enemy.

We may even *become* outsiders if we violate important rules. Teens might be shunned if they are perceived as too different. One might lose a driver's license for dangerous or drunk driving. Family ties can be severed over abuse or betrayal. One might be ignored, interrupted, or given the "cold shoulder" by workmates. Those who break the social contract with serious violations may be sent "beyond the pale"—whether to prison or to exile.

Personal boundaries are the most difficult to define and defend

Interpersonal boundaries are rarely as simple as the examples cited above. To begin with, the most difficult boundaries to define and to defend are not those between us and some enemy, but rather between us and those we love. We are obligated to our closest friends and relations, so it can be very difficult to draw the line with them. There should be a give and take to personal relationships, but we cannot give so much as to threaten our own safety or health—either physical or mental. We may love a person but disagree over values or behavior. Keeping a healthy distance through clear boundaries will allow you to preserve the relationship without becoming enmeshed in fights with no point or problems you cannot solve. Here are some examples of boundary issues within important relationships.

- We want to please our parents and make them proud of us, for example, but does that mean we should do whatever they expect? Should they be able to dictate our profession? Our marriage partner? Where we live? Should we sacrifice our family's security to repeatedly bail out a parent addicted to alcohol, drugs, or gambling?

- We expect to submerge some of our personal wants and needs in the give and take of a marriage, but how much cooperation is too much? Should a spouse control who we interact with and when? How we dress? What opinions we may express? Where we live or work? How we raise our children?

- It is normal and healthy for parents to put the needs of their children above their own, at least some of the time. We lose sleep to care for infants. We feed our children first even when we are hungry. We may stay in a job we hate because of the financial security or the health insurance it offers our children. But should we stay in that hated job so that we can afford a car for a teenager? Should we sacrifice to pay for college for a child when our own bills are unpaid? Should we deny ourselves a second chance for happiness after losing a mate because a child does not approve?

- We expect friends to be mutually supportive, but sometimes a friend can come to rely upon us too much or too often. Should we repeatedly allow ourselves to get sucked into someone's drama, when that person seems unable or unwilling to learn from mistakes? Should we continue to spend time with someone who is always critical, leaving us feeling depressed and worthless?

Clearly, there are limits to how much we should give to or sacrifice for those we love, but exactly where those boundaries lie is far from clear.

ENTRY 37

Sometimes someone important in your life really pushes your buttons. You may replay the same fights, never able to agree to disagree. What are you really fighting about? Could it be a belief or value issue?

How might you change the script? Perhaps you can choose not to share some differences of belief. Maybe you can agree not to talk about issues that always lead to fighting. (You may need to remove yourself to enforce this agreement.) Can you frame the issue as a belief that you cannot compromise on? (For example, you might insist on driving when the other has been drinking.)

Analyze a difficult relationship like this, in terms of how your establishing and enforcing boundaries might make it more bearable, limit it, or end it.

_____

_____

_____

_____

_____

_____

_____

_____

_____

_____

_____

_____

ENTRY 38

Looking back over my life, there were times when someone important to me tried to exert too much control over my behavior or beliefs. Was I sending mixed messages? Did I openly declare my boundaries or expect others to read my mind?

_____

_____

_____

_____

_____

_____

_____

_____

_____

_____

_____

_____

_____

ENTRY 39

Did you ever declare a boundary but not mean it? Sometimes, we say "No" but do not enforce it. Think back to a time when you allowed someone to invade a boundary like that. Were you using the "cover" of someone else's will to allow you to do something you really wanted to do? Were you giving in due to fear of rejection by the other person? Were you saying "no" only because you liked the attention and being chased?

_____

_____

_____

_____

_____

_____

_____

_____

_____

_____

_____

_____

_____

_____

ENTRY 40

I now realize there was a time in my life when I tried to exert more control over someone else than I should have. Here is what I did and why, and how it worked out. How would I handle this situation differently today?

_____

_____

_____

_____

_____

_____

_____

_____

_____

_____

_____

_____

_____

_____

_____

_____

_____

_____

When boundaries are violated

Defining and honoring personal boundaries affects the intimacy we share with family and friends. Respecting our and others' boundaries impacts the functioning and the effectiveness of classes, teams, organizations, and workplaces to which we belong. It also determines, to a great extent, whether we enjoy being part of them.

Often, teens feel lured or pushed to pursue dreams that are actually unmet goals or aspirations of influential adults in their lives. Being someone's protégé or favorite child, player, or student is not a completely positive experience. Many share that they believed their worth and value to someone they cared about was tied to their achievement and performance in the classroom, on the athletic field, or in the workplace.

Similarly, intimate relationships can impinge on our sense of wholeness and separateness. Someone in love might say that the beloved "completes me" or "makes me whole." Our very slang for a spouse—"my better half"—suggests that we are incomplete without that person. Even if that were true, would we want it to be? None of us is guaranteed a lifelong relationship, and even those must always end with the death of a partner. Is the partner left behind then doomed to a kind of half-life?

We each need to be whole persons. Only then are we able to have both intimate and respectful relationships with others. We can encourage and support one another but not push or force ourselves on others. We can be our individual and incredibly unique selves.

ENTRY 41

*Have you ever felt as if you were on some kind of achievement merry-go-round, where as soon as you won some prize or made some accomplishment, you had to set off in pursuit of the next one? Did a parent or teacher get so invested in your music or sports or artistic pursuits that you felt you could never quit or ease off without disappointing them terribly? Did you end up doing such activities for them instead of for yourself? How might you decide, if you had it to do over again, what **you** truly wanted versus what they wanted for you?*

_____

_____

_____

_____

_____

_____

_____

_____

_____

_____

_____

_____

_____

_____

_____

_____

_____

_____

_____

_____

ENTRY 42

The boundary between supportive coach or partner and co-dependent can be hard to draw. Have you ever, even with the best of motives, demanded too much from a child, spouse, or friend? What were the circumstances and why did you do so? Did things work out as you'd hoped, or was the person alienated by your overbearing attitude? Even if you got what you wanted, was it really worth it?

_____

_____

_____

_____

_____

_____

_____

_____

_____

_____

_____

_____

_____

_____

_____

Personal boundaries as expressions of ownership

Our body is the one thing we *know* is ours. No one else is responsible for understanding our bodies and our health. As the owners, that is *our* job. We cannot abdicate this responsibility to a doctor, a coach, or a celebrity endorser. If we really believe that nothing is more important than our health, do we act that way?

One way of turning beliefs into boundaries is to behave as if we take responsibility for our bodies. Establishing boundaries to protect our physical and mental health is like writing a personal owner's manual. For example, we might have clear expectations, habits, and support from a chosen few people related to our physical needs and health. We protect our schedules so we can get 8–9 hours of sleep at night. We exercise at least three times a week. We eat nutritional breakfasts and other meals. We carefully choose whom to be with so that these physical boundaries are maintained. We might have a friend who promotes working out or walking regularly. Another person may be our lunch buddy so we keep ourselves accountable for eating healthy meals and not running out for fast food. Someone else might join us in going grocery shopping or to the farmers' market and coming home to prepare healthy snacks or to cook for the upcoming week. We parcel out snacks and food in appropriate portions. Just think how much can be involved in simply trying to have some good physical boundaries related to health, exercise, and diet!

Notice from this example that boundaries take reflection, work, and follow-through. They must be well defined and attached to action plans. Here we see a belief in taking care of our bodies. We commit to making physical activity a priority in our daily lives. We demonstrate knowledge about our nutritional needs. We take action to buy, prepare, and eat foods that are good for us. And we recognize that we need support. We have a buddy or mentor to keep us accountable for living each day in a healthy way, either by participating with us or by simply checking in with us about progress toward our goals. Boundaries aren't short-term projects. They should be evident in our lives around the clock.

Defending these ownership boundaries

Just as we must establish our beliefs and values before creating boundaries, it also helps to think about our skills, interests, passions, and talents in terms of boundaries. Knowing what we are good at and capable of allows us to play appropriate and realistic roles in the various arenas of our lives. Not knowing allows us to be pushed or to push ourselves past our boundaries of competence or ability.

Think, for example, of athletes. They will have a certain amount of inborn aptitude and can develop their skills through practice. But gradual conditioning and focused practice is necessary to prevent injury. Working past the point of exhaustion does not add to competence and can also lead to injury. A coach who insists that athletes "play through the pain" is disregarding their personal boundaries in a way that can be dangerous.

A similar kind of coercion is quite common in school and work environments. A student who is in far over her head, where she cannot understand the work and is completely frustrated, is being pushed too hard. A worker who is promoted beyond his level of competence is being pushed too hard. A young woman who is pipelined into engineering studies because the field needs more diversity—regardless of her interests or skill set—is being pushed too hard. Even a cancer patient, who is told that a positive attitude and being a fighter are necessary for a good outcome, is being pushed too hard.

All of these boundary violations have one thing in common: they assume that determination is all we need to succeed. **We know that is not true.** Trying to run a marathon without steady and careful training cannot work. A student must master basic mathematics in order to handle higher math. Choosing or switching jobs or careers calls for both training and consideration of personal talents and skills. And a seriously ill patient is further victimized by the notion that illness is his fault.

Ironically, these trespasses on our individuality are rampant because our society so highly values the rugged individual with can-do spirit. You hear it in our common philosophy and mythology:

- There is no "I" in team.
- Perspiration is more important than inspiration.
- There's no such thing as second place.
- Winning isn't everything; it's the *only* thing.

While there is some truth in all these notions, they are also early warning signs of boundary violations. Teams actually are made up of individuals with differing roles and talents. Determination and hard work cannot overcome some limitations or barriers. Not everything in life is or should be a competition.

Self-awareness and self-respect will help us to see when we are being used for someone else's purposes, when we are being pushed too hard, and when we need to lay out and defend clearer boundaries.

We have ultimate control of what we do with and to our bodies. When we own our bodies, we have authority to determine where they go and with whom. We take responsibility for who we allow to touch us, how, where, or when. We know when we require physical distance from someone. We can set limits for what we will or will not do, or allow to be done to us.

Everyone has different external boundaries that need to be honored. For example, we are in charge of who we allow to give us a hug, kiss, or handshake. Every person has different comfort levels regarding intimate, friendly, or casual touch. No one is right or wrong for having their touch boundaries and limits. These are influenced by our culture and past experiences. Some of us are more "touchy-feely" than others. When we honor and respect our personal external boundaries, we are able to honor and respect those of others.

People from different cultures also have differing expectations about personal space. Some converse with little physical separation, while others would take that as "getting in my face." In some cultures, males commonly hold hands, but others see that contact as suspicious or wrong. Because these boundary expectations are taken for granted, their violation makes us feel subconscious discomfort. We may not know why we are on edge, but that unconscious reaction shuts down opportunities for communication. Making conscious and deliberate choices about boundaries can prevent this kind of misunderstanding.

Defined boundaries will guide choices about putting physical distance between ourselves and others. A person may bother you or send out "vibes" you don't like. You might choose to erect a physical boundary by removing yourself from the room. You might cross the street to walk on the other side. You might ask a teacher or boss to let you move your seat away from a person. Knowing our personal boundaries lets us take responsibility for ourselves.

Sexual and competency implications of boundaries

Possible sexual implications are an important aspect of boundaries. We are responsible to communicate and to give permission or non-permission for how we let others touch us. We need to clearly know our sensual or sexual touch boundaries in order to speak up and define limits for various people and in different situations.

Our dress and behavior can send sexual messages. We must consider how others receive those messages. Most of us would agree that sexualized dress is inappropriate for young girls. But women should also consider when and where exposed cleavage and sexy dress is appropriate for them. Do we always want others to perceive us in a sexual way? Might that not interfere with their estimation of our competence? Might it not lead to advances that are unwelcome? Might it not cut off some avenues of communication, since body language can be louder than voices? There is a fine line between presenting yourself as attractive and displaying your sexual attributes. This is clearly a boundary issue.

A similar issue for both men and women, without the sexual implications but with the same effect on their perceived competence, is casual dress. Although many places of business now allow casual dress all or most of the time, it, too, sends subliminal messages. People may subconsciously assume lack of competence when we are poorly dressed. Sometimes we must dress more formally in order to be taken seriously.

We must also realize that, at some times and places, we are *de facto* role models for others. A parent volunteer at an elementary school, for example, should not be wearing a tee shirt with an obscene slogan or cursing like a longshoreman. When we behave inappropriately like this, we are violating others' boundaries. If we expect to be treated with respect, we must show that same respect to others. Playing our various roles with due care is not the same thing as being a hypocrite. Rather, adapting our appearance and behavior to different situations and audiences is simply mature social behavior.

ENTRY 43

*Can you think of a time when your dress sent messages you had not intended? Perhaps you wore old or inexpensive clothing and a car salesman ignored you, assuming you could not be a serious prospect. Maybe you dressed to look "hot" but then got attention you did not like or did not get the job you were seeking. **Of course** everyone should be treated with respect at all times, but can you now see that others assumed things about you that you had not intended?*

_____

_____

_____

_____

_____

_____

_____

_____

_____

_____

_____

_____

_____

_____

_____

ENTRY 44

Trivial or minor violations of physical boundaries happen all the time. Someone cuts in line at the grocery or coffee shop. Someone takes the parking space you were waiting for. Someone rushes down the disappearing lane in a construction zone to get ahead of all the traffic that merged earlier. You know how you react to such violations — with annoyance, aggravation, or even fury. Are you ever the offender in cases like this? If so, why? Do you think that you are somehow special or more deserving than everyone else, that your time is too valuable to waste? Do you think others view your behavior in the same way?

_____

_____

_____

_____

_____

_____

_____

_____

_____

_____

_____

ENTRY 45

Think of a time when your physical boundaries with someone else were seriously violated. Our reactions to such violations can range from annoyance to anger to outrage, but perhaps the most destructive response is when we blame ourselves. Such reactions may stem from childhood abuse when we were blamed for the abuser's actions: "You made me mad!" We may have unconsciously accepted that blame, when in truth such violations are the abuser's fault and responsibility, not the victim's.

Are you carrying around this kind of childhood baggage? Can you now see these incidents as boundary violations?

_____

_____

_____

_____

_____

_____

_____

_____

_____

_____

_____

_____

_____

_____

_____

_____

_____

_____

_____

_____

_____

Mental or Internal Boundaries

Just as you sometimes must defend your body, you also must defend your soul. You do this with internal boundaries.

Internal boundaries allow us to control and take responsibility for our own beliefs, memories, thoughts, feelings, values, hopes, dreams, and passions. Internal boundaries are essential so that we allow others to be responsible for themselves, too. When we are keenly aware of and have solid internal boundaries, we do not try to invade others' internal space. We do not take responsibility for their behavior, ideas, decisions, or feelings. We honor their internal boundaries. Here are some ways to think about the complexities of internal boundaries.

- *Feelings* come from within us, and we determine when and how to express them.
- *Attitudes* about others — and ourselves — are our choices and totally up to us.
- *Personal behaviors* are our responsibility and not that of anyone else, even when or if we are under the influence of drugs, alcohol, or a swing of high or low feelings.
- *Words spoken* to others are our personal responsibility. We use words to put distance between ourselves and others. We also use words to let someone close.
- *Self-talk*—what we say to ourselves about ourselves—is our choice.
- Even *non-verbal expressions* are within our control.

Internal boundaries are complex and shifting. The above list simply provides a launching pad for us to think more about them. What are your internal boundaries related to limits, love, talents, passions, hopes, dreams, legacies, or how you use your time?

Without solid internal boundaries, we may become compliant. We let others have their way with us. We aren't able to say "no" or to say what we mean and mean what we say. On the flip side, we can become controllers who disrespectfully trample right through others' internal boundaries. We may become indifferent and non-responsive to others in our life. We might become self-absorbed and unable to care for and love another. We may become apathetic, avoid others, or be unable to seek help or advice. Many internal boundary troubles are possible and worthy of examination as we grow, develop, and lead our lives.

ENTRY 46

Simply put, boundaries define who I am and what my responsibilities are. Looking at the "big picture," it is helpful to think of examples and non-examples.

Examples of boundaries	Non-examples of boundaries
I am responsible for my own happiness.	I am responsible for your happiness. Or you are responsible to make me happy.
I am responsible for my behavior.	I am responsible for your behavior. Or you are responsible for what I do.
I own my attitude and outlook on life.	I am responsible for your attitude. Or you are responsible for my attitude.
I am responsible for my choices.	I am responsible for your choices. Or you are responsible for my choices.
I am responsible for my feelings.	I am responsible for your feelings. Or you are responsible for my feelings.

Add examples and non-examples of boundaries from your own life.

_____

_____

_____

_____

_____

_____

_____

_____

_____

_____

_____

_____

_____

Emotional boundaries

Feelings are so complex and so integral to our humanity that the next chapter or journey of this book is devoted to them, but it is useful to consider emotions in terms of the boundary metaphor. Emotional boundaries are crucial to controlling our interactions with and responses to others. With an examination and awareness of emotional boundaries, we can keep our distance or even disengage from others who are hurting or manipulating us. At the extreme, we can also realize when we are being neglected, being abused emotionally or psychologically, or allowing another person to control us emotionally. Sometimes we may see that we have thrown in the towel and become compliant to another's whims and desires.

Mental boundaries are not barriers to keep others out; they allow us the freedom to have our own ideas, thought life, and opinions. Underlying mental boundaries is the belief and value for every person being entitled to have freedom of individual thought. We should see a red flag when we find others trying to dissuade us from having an idea, passion, dream, thought, or opinion. Those persons are trying to invade or break through our mental boundaries to change us, to control us, or to manipulate us into their way of thinking. Who you are should be non-negotiable. Healthy relationships require respect for one another's mental boundaries.

Co-dependency can happen when we give up our mental and emotional boundaries, when we let another person take responsibility for our mental and emotional state. Or we may sometimes see ourselves or others becoming the

rescuer. This happens when someone jumps in to "save" or "fix" another person. The result is inadequate emotional and mental boundaries. We can become stuck on a slippery slope in these relationships without noticing that it is happening.

If we allow ourselves to be saved,

fixed or rescued, we avoid consequences. The tell-tale sign of impending trouble is when we no longer can express what we think or feel. We struggle to define ideas, opinions, beliefs, and values. We sense we are being taken captive when we are with the other person or group. We shut down — we can't be our true selves. We somehow allow the other person or group to push their beliefs, actions, attitudes, opinions, or values on us.

We are the only ones who can define, erect, and protect mental and emotional boundaries in our lives. Remember: **we cannot change anyone but ourselves**. We may not be able to stop others from trampling on our boundaries, but we can get out of the way. Sometimes we need wisdom and support to step back from some people in our lives to regain our mental and emotional boundaries — and to take back control of our lives. Boundaries liberate us to dream, hope, and care about ourselves and others. Boundaries protect our minds and hearts—the unique hopes and passions that reside in the deepest recesses of our being.

The authors are not counselors, therapists, psychologists, or psychiatrists. *Passport 2 Purpose* provides a springboard for more knowledge, skills, and decisions to make our lives more meaningful and joyful. If reflections along the way cause serious remorse, pain, anger, or fear, we may need to seek the counsel and advice of professionals. There are many who can help us when we need to identify personal boundary issues and problems, and to gain skills and strategies to develop and live out healthy boundaries.

ENTRY 47

With whom do you feel confident and secure? Describe with some detail the internal and external boundaries that are honored and respected between you. Why do you feel so trusting and safe with this person?

_____

_____

_____

_____

_____

_____

_____

_____

_____

_____

_____

_____

_____

ENTRY 48

With whom do you feel inadequate or insecure? Describe what is going on to cause these feelings. Have your internal or external boundaries been trampled? Have you communicated your boundaries to this person?

_____

_____

_____

_____

_____

_____

_____

_____

_____

_____

_____

_____

_____

_____

_____

_____

ENTRY 49

With whom do you feel charged, optimistic, and energized? What do you freely share with this person? Why do you feel so safe and free to share with this person?

_____

_____

_____

_____

_____

_____

_____

_____

_____

_____

_____

_____

_____

_____

_____

_____

_____

ENTRY 50

With whom do you feel pessimistic and downcast? What are examples of the conversations and experiences you have had with this person that left you feeling this way?

Are there boundaries for what you talk about, do, or share that need to be erected and respected to help you change what goes on when you are together?

_____

_____

_____

_____

_____

_____

_____

_____

_____

_____

_____

_____

_____

_____

_____

_____

_____

_____

_____

_____

_____

Signs of Boundary Trouble

Boundary issues are rooted in our earliest childhood experiences. As little children, we are like sponges as we watch how people interact, how people help one another or get their way, how people push their opinions and desires on others, when people pay attention to us, and what we do to get that attention. Children see what physical space belongs to whom. They know when people respect others' opinions, plans, hopes, and dreams. They see people who project their own ideas, values, and attitudes on others. We absorb these notions of how to behave and do not question them.

When parents and caregivers have healthy boundaries, children know roles within the family, see limits exercised, experience security, and grow in their own independence as fully whole and separate persons. Children see and internalize a model for healthy boundaries when their parents respect one another's individuality.

No family has the perfect setting or "story" of establishing healthy boundaries, but some are virtual train wrecks. When children grow up in an environment with little or no discipline, few to no consequences for emotionally or physically hurting others, few healthy boundaries lived out by either or both parents, the presence of alcohol or drug abuse, or the regular

witnessing or receiving of abuse or neglect in any form (verbal, physical, emotional, or spiritual), they will have boundary problems in their own lives.

Being controlled

Because we have soaked up these behavior habits and do not think about them consciously, we react instinctively to triggers from childhood. We can be put into full fight-or-flight mode and not even know why. Low self-esteem in adults reveals the battered and neglected child within. We cannot exorcise these demons until we recognize them. We can be ruled by fears we don't even realize we have. We experience discomfort and uncontrollable urges that, deep down, are residual fears. A few examples:

- *Fear of disapproval*—when we never or rarely say "no," disagree, or offer an individual idea, want, or need for fear that the other person will be displeased. In these relationships, we are hooked on trying to please others all the time. Or we yearn for approval at nearly any cost to ourselves.

- *Fear of being abandoned*—we may be afraid that someone will leave us or withhold their love and attention from us if we set boundaries with them.

- *Fear of being alone* — we are scared to be by ourselves. We avoid any disagreements or turbulence with someone because we don't want them to go away. We might become passive and allow others to make decisions for us because we want them stay with us.

- *Fear of being unworthy* of another's friendship or relationship. We may think we are unlovable. We have come to believe we are unlovely, unworthy, and undeserving of time, attention, care, or love from others. We may not stand up for ourselves with someone who is abusive or neglectful. We may be twisted in our thinking and believe that no one else would replace the abuser—no one else would love us or be our friend. We may feel unworthy to receive gifts, praise, or compliments from people in our lives.

- *Fear of being innately bad*—if we have suffered abuse, neglect, indifference, or ongoing apathy, we may believe we are a basically "bad" person or a "loser." We may have tremendous guilt about what was done to us or what we did to another person. We struggle with letting our "yes" be "yes" and our "no" really be "no." We may even say "yes" to someone when inside we are screaming out "no."

- *Fear of hurting another*—when we have been hurt deeply and regularly in our formative years, we may just expect to keep being hurt in our lives and relationships. Sometimes we think we can save others from being hurt. We try to fix and rescue others.

When we have deeply held and perhaps even buried fears, we may become compliant and let others control us. We allow people to push in or catapult right over our boundaries. Or we may simply give up being ourselves in order to please the other person or keep the peace in the relationship, family, workplace, organization, or team.

Being the controller

When we suffer from boundary problems, we may become controllers. Controllers simply do not respect the boundaries of others. A controller will try to take over and push ideas, wants, needs, values, hopes, feelings, or desires on another. We can be manipulative in controlling others by enticing, wooing, or cajoling them to do something they don't want to do. We may put a guilt trip on them. Sometimes we convince people to abandon their boundaries for just a while or even permanently to engage in the activity or relationship we want them to do with us. Manipulators are usually seducers. They know how to get someone to act, think, or do what they want of them. They know the right buttons to push at the right time to get a response. They know how to get under the skin and irritate the other person.

Some people are outwardly aggressive controllers. Such persons are abusive to others. They simply push through or trample over another person's boundaries to take or do what they selfishly want with them. When we are victims of such control, we are at great risk. These controllers rarely, if ever, will listen to reason or care about the feelings being experienced by the victim. Controllers generally think they don't have a problem, and so they won't seek or be open to professional help.

Time to get help

We are all capable of being both — controlled and controllers. These are two sides of the same boundary issue. Whether we fall into being compliant or being overly controlling, we need to recognize it and respond. When we are being controlled, we may need to seek another person's help to encourage us to take the steps necessary to escape it. If we try to force our needs, desires, and wants on another, we also need help to see what is happening and why. Bottom line: we *need* our internal and external boundaries in order to be ourselves.

ENTRY 51

As a child, teen, or young adult, I remember feelings that indicate there were serious boundary issues and problems going on. Here are my recollections of who I was with and what was going on when I had these fears.

- ***Fear of disapproval*** *— I tried so hard to gain approval when ...*

_____

_____

_____

_____

_____

_____

_____

_____

_____

_____

- ***Fear of being abandoned*** *— I was scared that this person would leave me....*

_____

_____

_____

_____

_____

_____

_____

_____

_____

_____

_____

_____

- *Fear of being alone* — I remember times when I was afraid to be by myself....

_____

_____

_____

_____

_____

_____

_____

_____

_____

_____

- *Fear of being unworthy* — I just didn't think that this person would like or love me because ...

_____

_____

_____

_____

_____

_____

_____

_____

_____

_____

- **Fear of being innately bad** — I felt horrible about myself or unworthy of having a relationship with this person who …

_____

_____

_____

_____

_____

_____

_____

_____

_____

_____

- **Fear of hurting another** — I remember feeling responsible for this person's feelings and happiness when …

_____

_____

_____

_____

_____

_____

_____

_____

_____

_____

_____

HEALTHY BOUNDARIES

Our Sphere of Influence

We are inherently social creatures, so our choices will almost always impact others. We all have a sphere of influence—individuals or groups that we observe and learn from—as well as others who notice and are influenced by us. We need to be reminded of the children, teens, family members, or colleagues who look to see how we deal with conflict, respect our bodies, encourage and edify others. We realize that we cannot change anyone else but ourselves, but we can influence, encourage, and support others to have healthy boundaries by reflecting them in our daily lives.

We are all role models for someone, whether we intend to be or not. Children absorb family behavior habits as "natural." Does our behavior replicate and pass on habits that we hated ourselves as children? Or do we break the chain of dysfunction? Teens watch what we do much more than they listen to what we say. Have we modeled the kindness, tolerance, honesty, and integrity we claim to value? Friends and coworkers, especially if they admire us, will emulate our behavior. Do we set a standard that elevates us all or that drags us all down?

We may not realize until much later, if at all, that we have profoundly impacted lives around us without knowing or intending it. A heartfelt scribble in a yearbook or conversation at a reunion may be our first clue that we once inspired someone or came to their rescue. Teachers and parents will hear years later that something they don't even recall saying (something wonderful or something dreadful) was etched into a child's memory, never to be forgotten. This power over others is an awesome responsibility. The people in our lives are always watching and judging our behavior. Would we be proud or ashamed of their verdict?

Influence works both ways

Just as we influence others, we are influenced by them. This is a boundary issue because we can choose who we allow to come close enough to affect us. We can choose our friends. We can choose how and how much to interact with our relatives and coworkers and neighbors. We can decide which celebrities to follow and imitate. Many of our beliefs and attitudes about boundaries were influenced by what we saw and experienced while we were growing up. If we are unaware of those subconscious attitudes, we may accept as "normal" conditions that are not in our best interest.

We need to be aware of which people in our lives bring out the best in us. Who lets us be ourselves? Who do we feel safe to be with and to share our ideas, dreams, plans, hopes, beliefs, hardships, frustrations, skills, and "life" with? Such people have clear and healthy boundaries and promote us having them, too. We feel secure, accepted, encouraged, genuine, respected, understood, and validated with such people. That does not mean that they will always agree with us or with our choices, but they will respect our right to make them.

When we are with people who have unhealthy boundaries, we tend to feel anxious, vulnerable, insecure, intimidated, judged, misunderstood, guilty, jealous, and even sometimes afraid to share an opinion, idea, plan, or belief that is different from the other person's. If you find yourself metaphorically tiptoeing around someone to avoid causing an upset, that is a warning sign that your boundaries have been trespassed upon. If you cannot comfortably be yourself with someone, that relationship is obviously not healthy for you.

ENTRY 52

As a child, teen, or young adult, I had people in my life who encouraged and let me "be me." I felt unconditional love from one such person as shown by the time when

_____

_____

_____

_____

_____

_____

_____

_____

I remember times when this person would just patiently listen as I shared ideas, hopes, passions, causes, interests, or feelings about someone or some situation. I felt really worthy and important when I was with this person, and I think it was because

_____

_____

_____

_____

_____

_____

_____

_____

ENTRY 53

Does my friend, partner, or parent insist on my behaving as he or she wants rather than doing what I think is right?

Is he jealous of the time I spend with other people or in activities that are important to me?

Do I find myself constantly trying to please her, or to win her trust?

If these conditions ring true, is this a relationship I should stay in? Am I at risk of losing myself?

_____

_____

_____

_____

_____

_____

_____

ENTRY 54

Who does not allow me to openly express my ideas, opinions, and personal beliefs and values? What are some examples of times we have been together when I was "run over" by her? Or when did this person or group push her ideas, opinions, beliefs or values on me? What boundary problems are there when we are together and I am trying to share "me" with him?

What am I going to do about seeing and spending time with individuals or groups that won't let me be myself?

_____

_____

_____

_____

_____

_____

_____

_____

_____

Boundaries of friendship in a new age

Few things have changed faster or more profoundly than the reach of friendship ties in an era of electronically facilitated social networking. Long ago, human interactions were limited by physical barriers: few people moved from the places where they were born. Even fewer did any extensive traveling. Americans are less rooted than most peoples, probably because most of us descended from ancestors who deliberately chose to leave their original homes. Today, we are very mobile. We move far—and permanently —from home as we pursue higher education or marry or take jobs. We move frequently for better housing or opportunities. At one time, moving away meant losing touch with family and friends.

No longer. Where once we may have exchanged a few letters or expensive long-distance phone calls per year, by the 1990s we were able to interact quite frequently via email. Then nationwide long-distance calling plans and personally carried cell phones allowed easy voice communication. Now we can follow the mundane details of daily living of as many people as we choose through Facebook and other such media, nearly as they happen. We are just beginning to realize the profound implications of this technology for boundaries.

To begin with, we are realizing that our expectations of privacy have been overtaken by events. Once we "Google" ourselves and find how much of our personal information is now part of a worldwide public domain, we understand that certain conditions have changed irreversibly. Now we must decide how to adapt our expectations and management of boundaries to these changed circumstances.

Are we revealing too much?

Many people are routinely horrified at how revealing others are on social networks. They will tell the entire world where they are going and when (even "checking in" at each destination), will share their most intimate or embarrassing experiences, and will even display revealing photos of themselves and others. They post and "tag" photos with others' names without getting

their permission first. They express any and every thought and opinion, often in language that shocks or appalls parents and employers. They complain about their workmates and bosses, threaten one another on line, and even post suicide notes and plans to hurt others. Parents track their teens through the GPS in their cell phones. They appear to respect no boundaries whatsoever.

Why is this so? It may not be entirely deliberate. We jumped into using these new capabilities without thinking through the consequences. Electronic communications promote a false sense of intimacy, even as they can be easily read or disseminated worldwide. Children will pour their hearts out in on-line forums and then be indignant if parents review what they have posted—as if there could be any expectation of privacy in this medium. Teens will recount in great detail how "wasted" they got over the weekend and the misadventures that ensued. Then they will be positively shocked that police agencies, court officials, and school disciplinary bodies will use that information to counter their later, sanitized versions of events. It never occurred to them that a college acceptance might be withdrawn or a job offer rescinded over something posted on their Facebook Wall. People do not think about enabling break-ins at their homes when they post their vacation plans for all the world to see. We do not foresee the misuse of personal information such as date and place of birth or family relations in identity theft or elaborate scams.

The technology advanced faster than our experience accumulated and our customs adapted to it. We were quickly in over our heads.

Who is really your "friend"?

One pernicious aspect of this technological revolution has been the cheapening of the concept of friendship. Young people will boast hundreds or thousands of on-line "friends," but what does that mean? Historically, friendship implied reciprocal ties: friends knew and cared for one another, and there were common expectations that they would support one another in certain ways. A friend did not gossip about you or sabotage your relationships. Friends made efforts or sacrifices to serve one another's needs. They certainly did not share compromising or embarrassing stories or photos with a potential audience of millions.

Parents and teachers note that many young people now appear to prefer interacting virtually rather than in person. Teens often text-message one another incessantly, but they seem to be losing face-to-face communication skills. Children used to develop basic listening and expression abilities through play. Now, much play is solitary or virtual. Children no longer spend hours fighting over the rules of their games, yet that was a valuable experience in negotiating boundaries. What will replace it? How will they learn to share, to get along, to follow rules, to solve problems, to deal with difficult people?

Family dinners used to be the occasion for sharing news and opinions. Participants learned what to say and how; children learned tact and self-control along with table manners. Sibling and parent-child boundaries were renegotiated almost daily. Where and how are these lessons to be taught and learned now?

And let's not forget that children cannot be cared for "virtually." They need real people with hands-on engagement to teach them to speak, to read, to dress and wash themselves, to cook, to perform household chores, to apply themselves to work or study with persistence. Polls find that what today's children long for more than anything else is attention—someone to notice and interact with them. Unless we heed their call for our attention, they may be doomed to disappointment.

How often do you give full attention to anything or—more importantly—*anyone*? Can you converse without checking your smart phone? Can you put aside whatever you were involved with when your child or friend or spouse wants to interact? Are you available to your work colleagues 24/7 but not to your family? If so, you have serious boundary issues.

Do you ever give full attention to *yourself*? We all deserve some private time to be alone with our thoughts. We encourage you to declare personal boundaries regarding technological intrusion. If you choose to make yourself available to the world around the clock, recognize that that is your *choice*. You can choose to negotiate such boundaries: to not answer the phone during dinner, to turn off the television when family members need to talk, to carve out some time to be alone every day.

This may sound like curmudgeonly grousing, but we urge you to consider these notions with open minds. We see a general shallowing and degradation of relationships in our society that could undermine the implicit social contract that acts to keep us all free, safe, and happy. If we lose our ties of kinship, friendship, and citizenship, we may devolve into the allegedly natural state that philosopher Thomas Hobbes called a "war of all against all"—leading to lives that are "solitary, poor, nasty, brutish, and short." Our social ties are fraying, but we can choose to strengthen them.

ENTRY 55

Have I ever posted something on a social networking site that caused trouble for me or others? What was it and why did I do it? Why was doing so a mistake?

_____

_____

_____

_____

_____

_____

_____

_____

_____

ENTRY 56

When I am with people I care about, do I give them the full attention they deserve? Do I pull out my cell phone at the dinner table? Do I ignore my spouse or child in favor of watching television or surfing the web? Do I think about how this behavior makes them feel and how it affects our relationship?

_____

_____

_____

_____

_____

_____

_____

_____

_____

ENTRY 57

Can I recall a time when I felt ignored or brushed off by someone whose attention I really needed? Or a time when someone selflessly put aside a book or turned off the TV or computer and focused on me when I needed that? How did these experiences make me feel? How did they affect that relationship?

_____

_____

_____

_____

_____

_____

_____

_____

ENTRY 58

Being "too busy" is a choice. You can set boundaries that honor your values. By not doing so, what are you sacrificing?

_____

_____

_____

_____

_____

_____

_____

_____

_____

_____

Evolution of Boundaries

Boundaries are not something you can "set and forget." They take work to define and maintain, and they will evolve over time as circumstances change. Our ownership and control in life should expand as we gain competency.

Children are protected from more freedom than they can handle, but their arena of decision-making grows along with their skills and judgment. We do not allow six-year-olds to drive cars, for example, but sixteen-year-olds are routinely granted that privilege. In recent years, as we recognized the importance of developing skills and judgment, most states have moved to a graduated licensing system that restricts hours of operation and number of passengers until more experience has been gained.

Late in life, we may find our sphere of independence shrinking once again. We may need to surrender some control—perhaps over driving or over our finances—to others. Renegotiating these boundaries with our adult children can be every bit as delicate and frustrating a process as when we had to loosen the reins on them as teens. Just as we may have had difficulty recognizing that our children were becoming independent, we may find it very hard to acknowledge that we have lost some of the competence required for full independence in our old age.

Getting stuck in immaturity

A quick look about us will reveal evidence of a growing problem in our society: too many people are not growing up as they should. Plenty of adults may look like grown-ups but seem incapable of acting with maturity. Examples of childish irresponsibility and incompetence surround us. People have tantrums on the highway ("road rage"). They name-call in place of reasoned argument (on talk radio and cable television, in on-line forums, even in Congress). They deny any responsibility for their own actions (drunk driving, compulsive gambling, abandonment of families). They have few qualms about cheating (underpaying taxes, forging credentials, smearing one another in political campaigns). They put their momentary personal happiness above any other goal or commitment.

What is going on here?

Actually, it would take another entire book to answer that question. But a simple description of the phenomenon—people reacting without thinking —reveals a nation of folks who do not know who they are and what they stand for. If we know and are guided by our beliefs and values, we will have sign posts on the journey of life. When beliefs and values are internalized and conscious, we are no longer in turmoil, forever agonizing on where to go and what to do. Everyday decisions about where to draw boundaries to protect our beliefs and values come much more easily. Rather than pursuing fleeting happiness, heedless of its cost to others, we experience the deep joy of a well-balanced, content, peaceful, and satisfying life.

ENTRY 59

Teens are notorious for their emotional outbursts. Subconsciously, they are trying to establish their own independence and individuality, but they rarely know how to break the boundaries of childhood with tact and finesse. It doesn't help that parents may not realize that they must renegotiate the boundaries between them as their children grow.

Can you recall an episode in your own or someone else's teen years that was unnecessarily confrontational or even hurtful? How might the teen have better set limits on the intrusiveness of the adult? How might the adult have better responded and adapted to the relationship changes that come with maturity?

_____

_____

_____

_____

_____

_____

_____

_____

_____

_____

_____

_____

ENTRY 60

Many of us face boundary issues when an adult child returns to move in with parents. It may be the holiday or summer stay-overs of a college student, or the student taking refuge after flunking out or during job-hunting upon graduation, or an older child dealing with divorce, single parenthood, or sudden loss of a job.

How can you negotiate to allow the adult child some dignity and independence and yet honor the parent's desire for privacy and concerns over safety? How can you partition household chores and responsibilities, as well as deal with money issues? Your relationship has changed, so your roles and interactions should be consciously adapted to the new circumstances.

_____

_____

_____

_____

_____

_____

_____

_____

_____

_____

_____

_____

_____

_____

ENTRY 61

*Perhaps you or a parent have dealt with shrinking rather than expanding
competency and control. Suppose your widowed mother must move from her
home of decades into a safer group living arrangement. Have you helped her to see
that her "independence" living alone comes only at great cost to the children and
grandchildren who must assist her around the clock? If she made the decision to
move and sell the house, did you interfere in rather than help with that process?*

*What beliefs and values underlie the desires and reactions of all involved? Are some
desires overstepping boundaries? How can you renegotiate the boundaries between
you while preserving everyone's self-respect and the relationship itself?*

_____

_____

_____

_____

_____

_____

_____

_____

_____

_____

_____

_____

_____

_____

ENTRY 62

Our lives are inextricably interwoven with those of others. Thinking about your life right now, is there a person you interact with where boundaries are poorly defined or not respected? What beliefs and values are you suppressing or ignoring to get along? How is your inability to interact honestly and effectively undermining your relationship? How is it influencing the lives of others who are close to both of you?

_____

_____

_____

_____

_____

_____

_____

_____

_____

_____

_____

_____

_____

_____

_____

Summary of Journey 2

Personal boundaries offer me safety and freedom within them.

They let me enjoy relationships without compromising who I am.

The most difficult boundaries to define and to respect
are between me and those I love.

My boundary issues likely repeat patterns absorbed in childhood.

My feelings around others indicate whether or not
we share healthy boundaries.

- Journey 3 -

Understanding Feelings

As a society, Americans have long tended to prize rationality and to prioritize thinking skills in our educational systems. We believe that conscious, logical, unemotional reasoning is the key to problem-solving and to successful lives. But we now know that our reasoning is *never* free of emotion, and that much of it is done subconsciously—it involves more reflex than conscious reflection.

If we are ever to live more consciously, more aware of what we are doing and why, we absolutely must explore and master our emotional life and faculties. The most important life decisions we ever make—whether to stay in school, who to marry, whether and when to have children, what career to pursue, who to choose as friends—are made more on the basis of gut feelings than logic. And those feelings stem from and are inextricably bound to our relationships.

Feelings are our own personal reactions to our experiences and to our interpretations of events and of the behavior of others. Two people can theoretically share the same experience but receive it in very different ways. Feelings are triggered subconsciously by our memories and by the influences of past experiences. It is precisely because our feelings arise from our subconscious minds that we can find them mysterious.

And that baffling quality may be one reason why we often ascribe their cause to others. An important principle about emotions is that *no one can make us feel anything*. No one else can or should make us happy. No one else is to blame for our anger. Feelings arise from within us. How we do or do not choose to respond to them or to act upon them remains our responsibility. We are in charge of what we do with our feelings. The catch is that many of us do not know much about feelings, so how can we be accountable for them?

If we do not excavate our past, uncovering important relationships and the feelings engendered by them, we can become stuck in a loop. We allow our subconscious feelings to push us to repeat the same patterns, without knowing why. Think of these loops as the sound track or play list of your life, endlessly replaying. You may need to remove old songs, add new ones, or even change the genre of this "background music"—by trying new things, meeting new people, or developing new habits.

Making the invisible visible

Exploring where our feelings came from and what triggers them today can remove much of their power to control our behavior. And never doubt that emotions do influence our behavior! We tend to act first, for reasons unclear to us, and create justifications later. We make decisions based upon feelings but then add a layer of rationalizations to "explain" our behavior. Even if you do not see this in your own behavior, surely you have experienced someone else coming up with after-the-fact reasons for doing something that were not mentioned at the time, the explanations becoming more elaborate with each succeeding argument. Humans are very good at this. Our conscious minds hate mysteries and seem designed to solve them—without ever confronting the truth.

Try this thought experiment. Think of a movie or a novel you really love, one that evoked very strong feelings. Perhaps it had protagonists who

- encounter adversity, lose faith and hope, but then emerge from hopelessness to find purpose again, or
- struggle with addiction, lose everything, then make a triumphant comeback, or
- sacrifice everything to save others, or
- make bad choices of friends or partners, suffer for it, and live on to create a better life, or
- buck tradition or bureaucracy or bad guys to help people in need, or
- strike out on their own and courageously begin a whole new life.

For some reason, you really identified with or were inspired by these characters. This is the power of *story*.

You cannot learn from the experience of others simply by way of their telling you the lessons they learned, because real learning has an emotional component. We *can* learn from others via a novel, play, or movie, because these stories immerse us in the emotional context of the experience. Stories resonate with us because we can feel what the characters go through and so learn from their experiences vicariously.

Stories are how we explain our lives to ourselves and learn from the lives of others. We are constantly writing our own life stories, although we are only dimly aware of that most of the time. Making the process of self-analysis more conscious and deliberate is a way of becoming authors of our life stories—rather than  allowing our subconscious minds to continue to ghost-write while we only pretend to be authors.

Once we become more consciously aware of feelings and their origins, they can become quite useful to us. An unexpected feeling can serve as a warning, alerting us to a situation that may be bad for us. Modern neuro-science is pinning down the many subtle and lightning-fast assessments we make subconsciously and think of as intuition or gut feelings. We all have this subconscious assessment routine running all the time and may do well to trust it.

Feelings are also very useful as potential motivators. If we note how we feel after doing something we should not—whether that is bingeing on junk food or exposing ourselves to unnecessary danger—we can leverage that feeling to resolve not to repeat the experience. Similarly, when we experience feelings of relief, compassion, pride, or accomplishment, we can determine to repeat the behavior that brought on those feelings.

First, however, we must delve deeply into where feelings come from.

Origins of Feelings

Have you ever felt as if your emotions were out of control? Raging anger, an obsessive crush, depression you can't snap out of, grief or elation that impairs your judgment? Really strong emotions can be overwhelming. They can take over our brains and our lives in ways that make us question how much free will and self-control we actually have. They can lead to poor decisions and can destroy relationships. They can debilitate our bodies through physical side effects. They can figuratively burn bridges on our life path, changing our direction in ways we cannot alter later.

Emotions, in other words, are something we must learn to understand and to manage, if we are to truly take charge of our lives and destinies.

The first part of that prescription—understanding feelings—is often taken for granted. But we have found, over many years of working with children, teens, and adults, that many of us cannot even say exactly what we are feeling. We do not seem to have the vocabulary to name our feelings. Then, even if we can name them, we often do not want to claim them: that is, we do not like to admit what we are feeling, or we try to "blame" our feelings on someone else. So, we must begin this journey into feelings by describing them, then learn where they come from, and finally learn how we might tame their ferocity and manage their expression.

Deeply buried emotional prompts

Our most intense feelings come from our deepest and most important relationships. Humans are born helpless and will always fear returning to that vulnerable state—*especially* if they were not cared for in that original period of dependence.

Our basic sense of security is rooted in knowing, at a very young age, that we were loved and would be cared for. People who did not experience this can spend a lifetime searching for it. We are surrounded by people who were wounded by the sense of abandonment and the lack of nurturing they experienced as children when left home alone or in child-care situations that did not meet their needs. Children of divorce may never get over the pain of abandonment by an absent parent. We all know someone who bent over backwards for years trying to win the approval of a critical and self-centered parent—and failed. We all know women who have repeatedly allowed themselves to be taken advantage of by men because they were seeking the father figure missing from their childhoods. We all know siblings who resent and compete with one another for parental attention—far into adulthood. Maybe we *are* these people. We must uncover and confront the buried emotions that impel us to act inauthentically or out of control, thus betraying our beliefs and values and damaging ourselves and our relationships.

Subconscious habits and tendencies can rule our lives without our ever realizing it. The key to changing the ruts in which we are stuck is to *see* them first. People can spend many years and a lot of money in therapy trying to uncover what makes them act as they do, but we can all accomplish a lot with considered reflection. Finding your true path requires commitment, effort, and — most importantly — taking time to be alone. We suggest that writing down your thoughts in a journal in order to clarify them is a method within reach of anyone.

ENTRY 63

Do you think that your parents or other caregivers gave you what you needed in childhood? Did you have to worry about where you would sleep or whether you would eat? Did you feel you had to earn your caregivers' love with good behavior? Was their behavior toward you unpredictable, overly critical, or even downright cruel? If so, how have the learned behaviors of that difficult childhood persisted in your adult life? Do you pander to significant others — trying to please them, to avoid upsetting them, to meet their expectations even when it is not good for you or does not align with your values?

ENTRY 64

Do you believe that babies and children deserve to be cared for selflessly by adults who love them? Have you been able to arrange this for the children you love? Have you sacrificed your own happiness, convenience, or priorities to put a child's needs first? Are you repeating parenting patterns that made your own childhood frightening and insecure? How could we, as a society, help to ensure that all children's basic needs for care and security are better met?

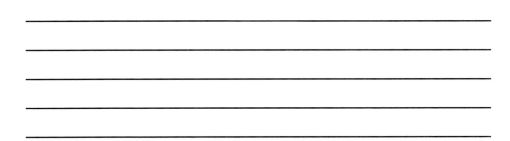

Clues to our critical memories

Here is a way to think about our past that can be helpful: noticing feelings that seem to come from nowhere and tracking them back to their origins. Years after the experiences that formed them, feelings may be reawakened by sensory triggers. Significant people and traumatic events have a powerful hold on our minds, but they are often buried in our subconscious. Sights, sounds, smells, tastes, and touches will bring back the feeling without awakening the memory. The feelings evoked are both strongly positive and strongly negative —these are the memories that linger. A touch, a smell, an accent, a melody, a photo, a familiar phrase—any of these can give you that *déjà vu* feeling of having been in the same position before. You may not be able to clearly recall what happened and when, but the feelings are replayed anyway. When has this happened to you?

The sight of a treasured mixing bowl will bring back the experience of making cookies with your long-gone mother. And accidentally breaking that bowl will feel like breaking your last tangible tie to a happy childhood. Seeing and using your late father's favorite coffee mug on a daily basis can make you feel close to him long after he's gone. Viewing photos in a frame or an album will revive long-dormant feelings from the best and worst of times. Consider the relics of deceased relatives that you hold onto: old tools, a shaving mug and brush, a watch, a piece of jewelry. You may not actually use them but, as tethers to your past, they invoke good feelings. Think of how you feel when seeing video of the Challenger exploding or of airplanes hitting the Twin Towers: it immediately brings back the shock, confusion, grief, fear, anger, and despair. Looking out upon a fresh snowy day can incite feelings of joy, playfulness, and excitement or of dread, depression, and fear. How do we feel when we walk near a homeless person with a sign asking for work or money; a couple having a picnic in a park; a family playing with children on a school playground; a parent reprimanding, disciplining, or spanking a child in a

store? Depending on our experiences, our past feelings, our moods, and even those we might be with at the time, we can have really different emotional responses to these situations.

Particular kinds of touch also awaken feelings. Brushing the hair of a bedridden, elderly woman may make her feel as loved and cared for as she did when her mother brushed her hair decades earlier. An inappropriately familiar touch will set off subconscious alarm bells in most people but may induce panic in those who were once abused. Jostling and bumping in a crowd can start fights as people interpret such contact as deliberately hostile. The feel of a puppy's paws on your leg can bring back the fear of dogs that began with one biting or knocking you down in early childhood. A warm and welcome hug can make you feel cherished and secure.

Familiar tastes, smells, and textures define "comfort foods." The smell of hot cocoa or a pot roast, or the taste of macaroni and cheese, can make us feel loved and happy. The odor of wet wool recalls the exhausting fun of childhood days of sledding and building snow forts. The smell and taste of hot dogs and peanuts elicits the feelings of excitement, belonging, and sheer joy we experienced at a baseball game. The smell of salty ocean air may bring an old sailor back to his youth—both the anticipation of starting a new journey in life and the fear, loneliness, and anxiety of war. A rescue worker who has dealt with burn victims may experience angst and fear aroused by the odor of a barbecue. Smelling sunscreen may evoke a vacation somewhere special. The aroma of wood smoke will induce the feelings we had when burning wrapping paper on Christmas morning or leaves in the fall, or roasting marshmallows in the fireplace, or making s'mores over a campfire.

Sounds, too, are keys to important memories. Think of how you feel when hearing the sound of an ice cream truck, a snatch of your favorite song, the crack of a baseball bat, music you once practiced for hours, the clang of thrown horse shoes, the honking and screeching that precedes a traffic accident, your old school's fight song, the scrape of shovels when sound is deadened by falling snow, the magnified sound of birds or of children playing in early-morning silence. Sounds are associated with previous experiences and call up the feelings we had during them. The thundering sound of monsoon rain on a metal roof will take the military veteran back to service in Southeast Asia. A cheering crowd can bring up the feelings of hope and triumph from a long-ago election-night victory. Anyone who has survived a tornado will react strongly to a similar train-like roar. A baby's cry or a child's "Mom!" will cause a woman whose own children are long grown to spring into action involuntarily. The sharp report of a backfire will cause a fight-or-flight response in a combat veteran.

Sometimes the triggers are vaguely familiar routines. An elderly man who waited in line in refugee camps during childhood, hoping the food would not run out before he got to the front of the line, may suddenly find himself panic-stricken in a grocery check-out line. A woman suffering from Alzheimer's dementia may suddenly become lucid and engaged around a cockatiel like her childhood pet. The right combination of sound, sight, and movement will call up "muscle memory" and associated feelings of triumph or dread from a once-practiced athlete or musician.

How do we feel when the alarm clock goes off in the morning? Some of us are refreshed, regenerated, and exhilarated about jumping up and facing the new day. Others are weary, overwhelmed, agitated, or anxious. Perhaps feelings are generated when we take in the sights and sounds of a bustling city from a crowded sidewalk. Some of us are excited and happy to have so many people around us. Others never feel quite so lonely as when amidst a crowd on a busy street, at a packed stadium, or in a mall full of shoppers. Or consider our feelings when we drive into the country or see a spectacular sunrise  or sunset. We can feel energized, awestruck, passionate, serene, spiritually connected, and refreshed by nature.

Most of us enjoy the good feelings evoked by associations with fond or positive memories. We have difficulty, though, when sensory triggers are linked to people, activities, and places where we experienced negative feelings like fear, insecurity, intimidation, vulnerability, anguish, shame, guilt, or physical or emotional pain. We felt bad because these experiences *were* bad for us. We were endangered or violated or used or let down by those we trusted and depended upon. That's okay. Bad things happen. The important thing is to learn and grow stronger from adversity. The danger is that, if we re-experience the feelings without understanding their origins, we can repeat the original bad experiences. Those echoes of bad childhood feelings can put us right back into the passive and vulnerable position of children. Instead, we need to recall and better understand the relationships, activities, and choices we made that were not good for us. We must figure out where our boundaries were violated and how we let our feelings or those of others control and manipulate us. Feelings are vital clues in our detective work about how we came to be who we are.

ENTRY 65

Think of some object that brings you feelings of comfort and quiet happiness: a photo, a piece of jewelry, a watch, a song, a family heirloom, some relic of your past. Why do you enjoy using or being around it? Are the feelings it evokes echoes of a warm and happy time of your life?

_____

_____

_____

_____

_____

_____

_____

_____

_____

_____

_____

ENTRY 66

Now think of a time when you suddenly felt strong emotions but could not figure out why. Perhaps someone used a word or phrase that immediately raised your hackles. For example: "Did you really do your best?" "I'll give you something to cry about!" "A thing worth doing is worth doing well." "What you meant to say was…." "You never listen!" "Don't you walk away when I'm talking to you!"

Maybe you astonished your companions with a vehement response to an innocent gesture or remark. What memory of something traumatic might be behind this over-reaction?

_____

_____

_____

_____

_____

_____

_____

_____

_____

_____

_____

_____

_____

Decoding the clues

Exploring our feelings can be like finding our way down a tortured trail. There are no signposts and the landmarks are obscured, so we must look very intently to see where we've been and where we're going. We need open hearts and minds to allow us to see and interpret clues. And, before we can analyze our feelings in this way, we must first be able to recognize them!

It can be surprisingly difficult just to name what we are feeling, especially if we are angry. Some experts say that anger is never a primary emotion — rather, it is a manifestation of other feelings. Any parent can accept this notion. Imagine your 16-year-old son has come home at 3 AM. You will likely be angry, but that anger stems from disappointment (that he let you down), fear (that he could have been in an accident or other serious trouble), and dread (that this is a symptom of substance abuse or the beginning of teenage rebellion). The child will often perceive only the anger and not realize that it demonstrates deep love, fear of loss, and worry about no longer being able to protect him as you once did. We rarely feel one thing at a time; dissecting and analyzing complex and conflicting emotions takes genuine reflection. Deciding how to express and deal with them should also be a deliberate and conscious process.

Before we can unravel the mystery of our own feelings, we must take inventory of them. We must notice what we are feeling and when. What are some feelings we seem to experience just about every day? Are we with others? Who are they? Where are we? What are we doing, seeing, or sharing? When, where, and with whom do we feel appreciated, comforted, confident, encouraged, energized, happy, hopeful, inspired, respected, serene, or uplifted? When, where, and with whom do we feel threatened, insecure, nervous, inadequate, stupid, despairing, hopeless, trapped, disrespected, or put down?

Once we take note of what we feel in what company and circumstances, we can begin to see patterns. And once we discern patterns—either negative or positive—we can choose to disrupt or to reinforce those patterns. We can choose to take a breather, to end a heated or hurtful interaction to allow time for reflection. Such a time-out can prevent us from damaging relationships while allowing for more productive interactions later. Postponing a conversation until we have cooled off is not denial or repression of feelings, but, rather, a way to honor boundaries and to live out our belief in respecting one another.

ENTRY 67 – NAME THAT FEELING!

An exercise that can help us to understand emotions is to brainstorm, alone or with a partner or small group, as many "feeling" words as we can. Generating a list of such words helps us to realize just how many, complex emotions we are capable of feeling. Here are some to get you started. Add your own to the list.

Annoyed	Anxious	Ashamed
Assured	Awed	Bitter
Brave	Calm	Compassionate
Content	Creative	Devoted
Exhausted	Energetic	Envious
Exhilarated	Excited	Forgiven
Frightened	Full	Happy
Honored	Hopeful	Humbled
Hungry	Intimidated	Introspective
Jealous	Loved	Lucky
Motivated	Naughty	Peaceful
Pitiful	Productive	Protected
Refreshed	Relaxed	Remembered
Respected	Sad	Safe
Serene	Threatened	Unhappy
Used	Valued	Vengeful
Violated	Wary	Worried

_____

_____

_____

_____

_____

ENTRY 68

Think of a time when you were in the grip of strong emotions. You were surely feeling more than one thing at the same time. Circle, on the previous list, as many of those feelings as you can; add any that are missing from the list.

What prompted these feelings? What had you just experienced that brought them on? Who were you with? What were you doing What were you looking at? What were you discussing? What were you thinking?

_____

_____

_____

_____

_____

_____

_____

_____

_____

_____

_____

_____

Why do you think these feelings were so strong? Have you ever felt this combination of emotions before? When and why?

_____

_____

_____

_____

_____

_____

_____

_____

_____

_____

_____

_____

ENTRY 69

Try writing a Feelings Journal or making a 24-Hour Feelings Chart. Record, at frequent intervals, exactly what you are feeling. Take note of where you are, what you are doing, and with whom. Once you have collected this data, analyze it for patterns. Then resolve to avoid the patterns that are bad for you and to encourage those that are good for you.

_____

_____

_____

_____

_____

_____

_____

_____

_____

_____

_____

_____

_____

_____

Feelings and Relationships

Because we are inherently social creatures, most of our feelings arise from relationships. When establishing new ones, we search for commonalities: experiences and connections and relationships we may share. When we are living through something terrible, awareness that we are not the first or not alone in that difficulty gives us heart. We know that, if others survived an experience, then so can we. Losing relationships—whether through voluntary or involuntary separation—is painful, because even dysfunctional relationships are important to us.

We are programmed from conception as social beings: babies *in utero* are significantly affected by their mothers' behavior. Babies possess an astonishing ability to read facial expressions—because relationships are so vital to our survival. We *need* others. But, as we grow older, we can exercise more control over who we are in relationship with. Babies cannot choose their parents, but our choices of friends, colleagues, and family expand with age. And every loss of relationship is an opportunity to choose the next one wisely.

Warning: you may actually limit or lose some relationships as you discover and define who you are and how you want to live. There is no point, after all, to having a choice if you never exercise that option.

Defining "relationship"

Relationships run the gamut from intimate to family to neighbors to community to society. We are always interdependent, although the balance shifts over time—from the total dependence of the baby to the interdependence of adults to the renewed dependence of the sick or disabled or elderly. One thing all relationships have in common is that they are two-way or reciprocal; both sides give as well as receive.

Some relationships can be very instrumental, with a what's-in-it-for-me? focus. They will serve a specific purpose and then end. If they are not truly reciprocal, they cannot last. That is why the unremitting takers, who seek and feel entitled to constant hand-outs, are eventually driven from the good graces of families and societies. They are not holding up their end of the tacit bargain we all make to give when we can and to receive when we must.

Consider for a moment how you feel when you are on the receiving end —of a compliment, a favor, a gift, a loan, or even the very personal services required by the ill or disabled. Does "taking" make you uncomfortable? Would you not prefer to be on the "giving" side? We believe that this common unease about receiving is rooted in how vulnerable we can feel when not in control. In fact, this whole book revolves around striking a balance between taking control of our lives and ceding control in relationships. Defining and maintaining that balance allows us to live purposeful and satisfying lives, but finding the happy medium is a lifelong project.

Our fear of loss of control is both ego-driven and unrealistic. We are never completely independent and completely in control. Nor, if we are honest about it, would we want to be. For those who believe and act as if they owe nothing to anyone are deeply unhappy people. They are denying their essential, social nature.

The concessions we make in enduring relationships pay off for us in security. Committed relationships require us to be vulnerable, by revealing our true selves, but they offer us the freedom to *be* ourselves, warts and all, and know that we will not be rejected or abandoned. Siblings, marriage partners, and close friends, when in healthy relationships, have in common the knowledge that the relationship cannot be torpedoed—that the other will continue to love them "no matter what."

So why are such enduring relationships not more common? You must experience such a mix of vulnerability and security at home before you can extend it to other arenas—and many of us did not. The reason this book has as many blank journal lines as lines of text is that *you* must excavate your life's debris. Where did it all go wrong? You were probably so young that you were in no way at fault. Certain life lessons you should have learned very young may never have been taught.

Recent research documents that persistently amoral juveniles, who repeatedly hurt others with no guilt or remorse, overwhelmingly come from homes where they experienced harsh discipline and no love. How were they to learn empathy if it was never demonstrated toward them? Your childhood care may have been much less inadequate than that, but did it give you the love and security every child

should have? Did you believe that your parents or caregivers would love you no matter what and never abandon you? If someone important bailed out on you, you had no model for persistence and commitment. If you missed out on the unconditional love that should be every child's birthright, you will have to learn these ways deliberately as an adult rather than by absorbing them unconsciously as a child. You can still do it, but it will take conscious thought and effort.

ENTRY 70

Think back to a time when you felt abandoned or betrayed by someone you counted on. Who was this and how did their actions make you feel? Do those feelings linger today? Since you cannot change the past, is there some way you can let this betrayal go and move forward to make the rest of your life more to your liking?

_____

_____

_____

_____

_____

_____

_____

_____

_____

_____

_____

_____

_____

_____

ENTRY 71

Describe an important relationship you would like to have — as a parent, sibling, partner, friend, grandparent, etc. How would this ideal relationship be different from relationships that have disappointed you? How would **_you_** _be different? Are you giving enough to the other? Perhaps more importantly, are you asking enough? Sometimes, when we are starved for love, we do not demand real reciprocity. Should your standards be higher?_

_____

_____

_____

_____

_____

_____

_____

_____

_____

_____

_____

_____

ENTRY 72

Many of us feel wounded or deeply insecure, since our society did not make the care of children a priority. This trend continues to accelerate. How can we change society *for the better, so that children grow up with the security that allows them to thrive? What small changes — such as being there for kids in your family or volunteering to help children in your community, company picnics, church celebrations, family reunions — might you make within your own inner circles that could ripple outward? Are there ways you can bring back the extended family and social interactions that used to weave a web of support around children?*

_____

_____

_____

_____

_____

_____

_____

_____

_____

_____

_____

Feelings about ourselves

Even our feelings about ourselves have been shaped by the opinions of others—for good or ill. Most of us adopt a role early in life that is crucial to our sense of identity, and that role was usually imposed by others. An obvious example is the very attractive person who has been recognized and praised for his or her looks. When your self-worth is inextricably bound to appearance, you will inevitably have trouble aging gracefully. We all know women who have increasingly drastic cosmetic surgery or men who dye their hair jet black in old age, seemingly unaware of how ridiculous they can look. But the saddest part of such attempts to hold on to youth is that they clearly feel that their value as persons hinges on such an ephemeral attribute as youthful good looks.

Even people who were not unusually attractive can have similar hang-ups about appearance. It is extremely common for women to share stories of hearing their own fathers routinely critique the appearance of women, giving the not-so-subtle message that looks are the most important thing women have to offer. Sometimes the message is brutally direct: "Don't ever get fat"—or else what? You won't be lovable or worthwhile?

Other children adopt identities as athletes or musicians, practicing long hours every day, year after year. Parents may intend only to be supportive of their children's interests, but children can pick up the message that they are valued for their physical skills. What happens if they lose interest, or want a more balanced life, or are injured and unable to continue? They may feel worthless and like failures, even when most of their lives are still ahead of them.

Some children, who live with a parent or other significant adult who is prone to depression or just unhappy with life choices, can fill the role of cheerleader. They may feel that a depressed person's life is in their hands, that only they can keep that person from suicide. This is a burden no one should carry, let alone a child. They may feel compelled to be bouncy and bright, to make others happy. Making others happy should not be one's purpose in life. For one thing, that outcome is not under our control; for another, that goal is not worthy of our potential greatness. We can be and do far more.

In families blighted by alcoholism or some kinds of mental illness, it is common for one child to adopt the persona of peacemaker. This can involve moderating the behavior of others so as not to set off the mercurial family member, or trying to placate the addict so as to avoid blow-ups. Trying to ensure that not only you but everyone else in the family walks on eggshells all the time stunts emotional growth. It prevents one from growing up and assuming adult control, since life is lived on someone else's terms.

Some who live with abuse at home keep up a front in the outside world, perhaps to protect the abuser from discovery, to try to feel "normal," or because they are ashamed to be living like that. It is extremely stressful to hide important parts of your life, to pretend to be what you don't think you are, to take on adult responsibilities as a child. Home is not the safe haven it should be.

Many children of divorce can be thrust into the role of friend and confidant to a parent. They are forced to take sides, demonizing the other parent. They are consulted on matters beyond their maturity level. They are robbed of childhood. All of these scenarios are damaging and can drive chronological adults to act emotionally like children.

Another common role is for the intellectually talented to find a sense of self-worth only in academic or leadership achievements. Such achievement is not a bad thing in itself, but using it to bolster your identity is ultimately unsatisfying. Can you ever rest on your laurels, or must you constantly chase new ones to prove that you are "good enough"? If you internalize the idea that you are much smarter than others, might you feel entitled to be in charge and become a master manipulator? Might you eventually think that the rules do not apply to you?

Some high-achieving teens learn early to play roles that look good on a résumé: volunteering in soup kitchens or organizing food drives or fund-raising for charity. Good things can be done for the wrong reasons: for ego strokes or the admiration of others. Would they give so freely if it were anonymous? If they are authentic actions, they should touch the actors and have real consequences for their lives.

Some people who have grown up very poor and somehow made it into a higher "class" will forever feel like impostors. Keeping up appearances and worrying about what the neighbors will think are their guiding principles. How stultifying such confines must be! Such other-directed folks are essentially saying that their worth is completely dependent upon the opinions of others. Again, that is ceding to others power that should rightfully be your own.

There are many varieties of family and group roles we may unconsciously adopt: the class clown, the loyal sidekick, the party animal, the one who will take abuse, the sympathetic shoulder to cry on, the first-born achiever, the baby of the family who is both neglected and not allowed to grow up, the shy one who will never stick up for herself, the dependable one who will clean up others' messes, the one who is always the good-natured brunt of another's jokes, the only child or eldest child who is given too much responsibility, the Good-Time Charlie, the favorite or pet, the rebel who follows no rules.

Choosing our roles

We all play different roles with different people and in different situations. We moderate our dress, speech, and level of frankness so that we are acting appropriately. But we should be aware of when we are being typecast—acting as others expect even if it does not serve our own needs.

Childhood roles, rooted in the expectations of others, only have power over us when they are unquestioned. The way to remove their power is to analyze the beliefs that underlie them. For, make no mistake, these expectations betray beliefs and values. They pigeonhole us in ways that are very limiting, asserting that we have value only so long as we look great, get all A's, are top-tier athletes or musicians, or can control the feelings and responses of others.

The ways in which we were valued when young strongly influenced what we value in ourselves, as well as the shortcomings we perceive in ourselves. We subconsciously strive to achieve the ideals that were held up for us. We allow our sense of self-worth to be rooted in what *others* value in us. If we want to escape the uncomfortable feelings that are a legacy of our childhood, then we need to step out of those childhood roles. We can choose to live out our chosen beliefs and values by enacting new roles.

Let's consider for a moment the concept of "value" in terms of "worth." We assert that every person has inherent value and dignity. We *are* more than what we can *do*. Our true value is derived from the values we claim and live out. Do we contribute to making our home, neighborhood, society, and world better places? Do we "pay forward" the advantages and favors we have been granted? Do we treat others with respect, dignity, and compassion? Do we give as well as take? Do we add value to the universe?

We should recognize and nourish our individual skills and abilities, but to what end? Is our end goal to be the best, the richest, the most famous? If we were to achieve any of those superlatives, would it actually satisfy us? There is nothing objectively wrong with excellence, but human beings are multidimensional, need balance in our lives, and can best find the purpose that fulfills us when we choose our own beliefs and values — and choose to live in accordance with them.

ENTRY 73

What was your own primary role as a child? Do any of the descriptions above resonate with you? When did you realize you were playing that role? (Or have you yet?) Why did you need to outgrow it?

_____

_____

_____

_____

_____

_____

_____

_____

_____

_____

_____

_____

ENTRY 74

What was your role in your family or with friends when you were a teen or a young adult? Why did you take on that role? Who were the people influencing you? How did they wield their influence over you? What beliefs and values do you think they had? What did they really want from you?

_____

_____

_____

_____

_____

_____

_____

_____

_____

_____

_____

ENTRY 75

Reflecting back now, what beliefs and values do you want to claim as your own today? What kinds of emotions should naturally arise within you as you live out your beliefs and values? When do you betray your beliefs and values? What feelings do you experience when that happens?

_____

_____

_____

_____

_____

_____

_____

_____

_____

_____

_____

_____

_____

Consider the source of criticism

Our most self-critical thoughts are often not ours at all. We can feel guilty, ashamed, and inadequate because of long-ago bad experiences. The feelings engendered by those experiences have power over us because, in some way, we have accepted the verdicts of others. "You are so stupid!" "You will never amount to anything!" "No one else will ever love you!" "I wish you'd never been born!" Such callous and spiteful verbal abuse illustrates what a lie the old adage "Sticks and stones may break my bones, but words will never hurt me" really is. Words *do* hurt. They wound deeply. The cruelest words are never forgotten.

One way to remove the power of harsh words is to consider their source. Why would we ever assume that someone's assessment of us is accurate? Look behind the words to see the beliefs and values they express. Was someone putting you down to build himself up? Was she trying to control or manipulate you? Was he destroying your self-esteem so that you would be afraid to leave? Were there generations of a dysfunctional family legacy behind the person's behavior?

Parents may see their children's behavior and accomplishments as a reflection of their own value and worth. Thus, they may be embarrassed when a child does not live up to their expectations, even if those expectations are unreasonable. If you were made to feel like a failure or an embarrassment by a parent, consider how wrong it was for that parent to try to live vicariously through you, or to impose such values and expectations on you. Your boundaries were violated by someone you loved and depended upon, so of course it hurt you. But that does not make it right. The blame lies with the parent, not you.

Such overstepping is really quite common in families. Think, for example, of deathbed promises extracted to remain in the religion of one's birth, to maintain the family farm or business, to care for a disabled sibling for life.

Outside of nuclear families, there are plenty of cases where others have unreasonable expectations and judgments of you that should be ignored.

Teenage boys might say that engaging in sex is proof of love or that you are not just a tease. Girls may say that expensive gifts are proof of love or that you are not just cheap. Employed mothers may denigrate the worth of stay-at-home moms, while the stay-at-homes call the "working" moms selfish. Molested children will be told they brought it on or are to blame. Someone will say, "I know you won't let us down" when the expectation is out of line. Or, they say it to manipulate you through emotions when they know you already have disappointed them.

The bad feelings others engender often stem from illegitimate demands. If the persons who hurt you did not have your best interests at heart, why not discount their opinions as completely unreliable? You know yourself better than anyone else does. You have the power to change who you are at any time. Do not cede that power to others by letting their judgment of you matter.

ENTRY 76

What are some unkind words spoken over you that still linger in your memory? Why do you think they were said? Do you believe them today?

_____

_____

_____

_____

_____

_____

_____

_____

_____

_____

_____

ENTRY 77

Reflect back on some really hard times in your life. All of us have survived difficult, even terrible, things. When we try to suppress those memories, we are also robbing ourselves of the opportunity to recognize our own growth. How has a bad experience made you stronger, more resilient, or more capable? How have hard times made you who you are today?

_____

_____

_____

_____

_____

_____

_____

_____

_____

_____

_____

_____

_____

_____

Feelings we engender in others

To be clear from the outset: we are not saying that you are responsible for what others feel. We do believe, however, that it is useful in our life journey to pay attention to how others feel when they are around us.

Feelings—both pleasant and unpleasant—can be infectious. Maybe we have been really sad, or angry, or depressed. A friend drops in or calls unexpectedly and shares some good news. Suddenly we smile and forget our own bad feelings. Hearing from them and knowing they wanted to share their happiness with us moves us to feel cared for, needed, worthy, and special. Or maybe we work with or are friends with someone who is consistently downbeat and cynical: everything and everyone in life seems to be disappointing. We may catch that attitude, or find that we really don't want to be around this person.

Imagine that a coach pulls a player to the sidelines just after he misses a shot, commits a foul, or loses the ball. Coach wraps an arm around the player and says, "It's okay. I believe in you. Get back in the game and have fun." The player feels relieved, forgiven, and a sense of confidence to get back in with the team.

A parent sees a child spill a glass of milk with no yelling or swearing or frantic moves to quickly sop up the mess. The parent grabs the roll of paper towels and says, "No problem, no worries, we'll just soak this up." The child's fear and stress subsides and instead he feels accepted, forgiven, and able to fix his own mess.

Perhaps a relative always offers unsolicited advice and criticism. We always feel we are being judged and found wanting. Even if we do not take this criticism to heart, we still feel uncomfortable around and prefer to avoid the critic. Another relative always seems glad to see us, to have plenty of time for us, and to be interested in our lives. We feel accepted, loved, and valued. We enjoy spending time with someone who sends out such subliminal messages.

We all have the power to influence the feelings and emotions of others coming in and out of our lives each and every day. Simple gestures, solid eye contact, a touch of the hand, a pat on the shoulder, or a few spoken words of assurance can help us feel connected, encouraged, hopeful, and happy. When others experience positive emotions in our presence, those feelings are reflected back and magnified. We both benefit. The choice of what to send out and receive back is up to us, every day.

ENTRY 78

Sometimes we spew bad feelings all over the nearest handy target — especially if that target is somehow powerless to resist the attack. Can you recall a time when you took negative feelings out on someone else who had nothing to do with why you were feeling bad or angry? Why did you do so? Did you apologize and atone for it? Have you resolved not to let it happen again?

_____

_____

_____

_____

_____

_____

_____

_____

_____

_____

_____

_____

ENTRY 79

When did someone violate your boundaries in this way, expressing anger or disgust at an inappropriate time or place or in an unjustified manner? Why do you think they did so? How might you have escaped or defended yourself better? Did you blame yourself for it happening? If so, can you now see that their feelings and actions were not your fault?

_____

_____

_____

_____

_____

_____

_____

_____

_____

_____

_____

_____

_____

_____

_____

ENTRY 80

Recount a time when your good feelings spread to others or theirs to you. Was this an experience worth repeating? How might you make it a habit?

_____

_____

_____

_____

_____

_____

_____

_____

_____

_____

_____

_____

_____

Chasing happiness

We cannot talk about relationships without discussing the way they are cavalierly discarded in the pursuit of happiness. Happiness and relationships should be entwined, so what is going so wrong? We must think about the nature of happiness in order to dissect this problem.

It is almost a cliché for American parents who consider themselves selfless to say they don't care who their children are or what they do "as long as they are happy." We consider this a step forward from previous generations, who may have had very definite ideas about how their children should behave and who they should become as adults. In fact, it *is* a step forward to acknowledge that our children have the right to choose their own selves and lives, since they are independent individuals and not simply appendages of their parents. However, is the goal of happiness for them enough?

The impulse behind that goal is good: we want them to live in a way that is not unnecessarily difficult for them. Meeting the expectations of others rather than your own will certainly make you unhappy. But we believe that happiness is a shallow and unsatisfying life goal. Life, after all, is difficult. We must all work to survive, and that work will often be more draining and less satisfying than we might hope. We will inevitably suffer illness, loss, injustice, and simple vagaries of fate—such as an encounter with nature's wrath or a drunk driver. Bad things *will* happen to us, and we cannot always be happy.

Also, one often hears irresponsible adults claiming that they "deserve to be happy" when they are ignoring how their choices affect others. Getting married and having children both necessarily imply duties to others. Of course there are situations when one must escape from an abusive relationship or eventually give up on a dysfunctional one. But such decisions should never be taken lightly. And one's obligations to minor children should never be abandoned. Even uprooting one's family for a job opportunity can be very damaging and should be thought out carefully.

Too many biological fathers completely forsake their children, relegating them to lives of physical and emotional deprivation. Many parents run out on spouses and children to pursue a "love of my life," seemingly unaware that they chase a series of such alleged once-in-a-lifetime opportunities. They allow hormones and selfishness to override social obligations.

We should restrain ourselves and reflect before jumping into the interdependence of relationships. A relationship is not just about "me," or even just about "you and me." Every relationship we join is really a network of relationships. You do not marry a person alone, for example; you marry into a family. Your desires may spring from your subconscious mind, but you can override them. Think carefully about what you want in a relationship before diving in. Shipwrecks are most easily prevented *before* encountering storms.

Happiness versus joy

The feeling we call "happy" tends to be circumstantial, lasting only as long as the situation does not change. The most overpowering happiness is rooted in primal, hormonal reactions that literally *cannot* be sustained. It is somewhat understandable when teens in the throes of a first love are unable to think straight; they've never been through this overwhelming experience before. When supposed adults behave the same way, they are betraying unworthy beliefs and values: that their own fleeting happiness trumps social responsibilities, that it is okay to abandon commitments if you think something better has come along, that collateral damage to your own children is acceptable.

There is a word for such self-centeredness: narcissism. It implies vanity, egotism, self-absorption, conceit, selfishness. Do you really believe that you are so much more worthy than everyone else, that your desires should always come first? When you have pursued your own happiness in these ways, has it brought you lasting contentment? Most of the good feelings in our lives do stem from relationships, which rarely last if they are one-sided, selfish, and superficial.

Happiness is fleeting and usually self-centered. Joy is more lasting and other-focused, usually involving the sacrifice of time, money, or effort. The deep contentment of a long-married couple springs from decades of mutual molding. The couple give and take, adapting to one another's needs, buoying each other through seasons of struggle and sorrow, taking solace in the reliability of their interdependence. A selfish concern with individual happiness would never allow them to reach this exalted plain of human relationship. Giving to others can be more rewarding than getting something for ourselves, because we were designed to be social. We can find deep joy and satisfaction in a life that consistently works toward achieving unselfish purpose—the purpose we choose for ourselves.

ENTRY 81

When did someone's selfishness hurt you? What happened? Why do you think the person behaved that way? What values did that behavior reveal?

_____

_____

_____

_____

_____

_____

_____

_____

_____

_____

_____

_____

_____

_____

_____

_____

ENTRY 82

When did you put your own needs and desires ahead of others' in a way that hurt them? Why did you do so? What values did this behavior expose? Did things work out as you had thought they would, for you or for those you hurt?

_____

_____

_____

_____

_____

_____

_____

_____

_____

_____

_____

_____

_____

_____

_____

_____

_____

_____

Managing Strong Emotions

We have explored where our feelings come from and how they will arise whether we want that or not. It helps a bit to understand their origins, as making this connection explicit tends to rob them of some of their power. It is helpful to realize we can choose to avoid some people and situations that we know will make us uncomfortable. But the very strongest negative emotions —terror, guilt, regret, grief—require something more than simple insight or avoidance strategies. They must be faced and conquered head-on.

There are certain feelings we must learn to handle by ourselves, through experience. That obsessive first love, and the overwhelming fear of loss of the beloved, is one. The grief of losing a sibling, parent, child, or spouse is

another, although each successive loss will be easier to bear than the first, simply because it is no longer unexplored emotional terrain.

This phenomenon — that even intense feelings are somewhat easier the second time around — is a clue we should heed. Novelty, fear of the un-known, and dread about just how bad an experience will be all serve to intensify emotions that are already naturally strong. These in-tensifiers are rooted in our insecurity, our fear that we will be unable to handle what is coming. Knowing that we have survived a "baptism of fire" once gives us confidence that, no matter how awful it is, we will make it through another such experience. This is why older people generally operate on a more even keel. They have been through a lot of experiences and know, personally, that they are survivable. They realize that hysteria and histrionics are a waste of energy: they intensify feelings and solve nothing.

Making peace with the past

We need not wait for old age, however, to resolve our unfinished emotional business. First, we must give up the idea that we can somehow make ourselves *not* feel something. If we were able to shut down this dimension of our personality and identity, that would cause more problems than it solves. Suppression of strong feelings does not work: they will emerge, one way or another. But while we cannot control how and what we feel, we *can* manage the expression of our feelings.

For some of us—those who need to feel "in control" to be comfortable—simply giving ourselves permission to feel negative emotions, such as grief or guilt or fear, can be a big help. As long as we insist to ourselves that we should "get over" some experience and no longer feel the way we do, those feelings will persist. Letting go of the illusion of control will finally allow the emotions to ebb. Simple "tincture of time" will gradually soften our pain if we let it.

For others, it is a tendency to wallow in emotions, rather than to deny them, that gets us into trouble. Allowing oneself to wallow in anger, for example, only intensifies it. We build up a big head of aggrieved and self-righteous steam, rationalizing away any contribution we ourselves may have made to a bad situation. There was a time when adults thought it was a good idea to teach children to take out their anger by punching a pillow, for example, but that kind of "solution" actually tends to make the child angrier, rather than releasing the anger as we had hoped.

In either case, where we need to get rid of negative feelings somehow, there are much better techniques than denial or full immersion. Loving relationships are the antidote for most of what ails us emotionally, but meditation, prayer, or progressive relaxation techniques can also help us to deal with debilitating feelings. The simple expedient of counting to ten or waiting 24 hours can be surprisingly effective in preventing us from doing or saying the wrong thing under the sway of feelings. Allowing ourselves to feel the full force of grief for limited but regular periods of time can help us to be functional the rest of the time. Regular exercise has been shown to improve depression symptoms and to relieve stress. Music can be a powerful way to experience and then purge strong emotions. Even interaction with a pet has been proven to relieve stress and negative emotions.

When we know the feelings will be with us for a while, we can take precautions to protect our lives from their side effects. It is important to avoid making critical decisions while under their influence, since feelings can literally impair judgment. That is why widows and widowers are advised not to make irreversible decisions, such as selling a house or remarrying, during the first year after the loss of a mate. Strong feelings—grief, despair, sadness, elation, euphoria—can be overwhelming. Giving ourselves some time for them to dissipate before taking unnecessary actions is wise.

Second thoughts about recurring emotions

Sometimes strong emotions haunt us. Recurring negative or troubling feelings are a common problem after some traumatic or deeply disappointing experience. How can we deal with them? First, acknowledge the feelings. Ignoring or stuffing them down hasn't worked, has it? Name them and write a little account of what was going on in your life when they first emerged.

This kind of journal-keeping is a very effective way of clarifying your thoughts. Then you can look back, probe and come to some understandings about these feelings. What prompted them? If you could travel back in time, knowing what you know now, do you think the feelings might be different? Or might you choose to perceive and experience them differently? Can you then focus on any positive or even neutral feelings? Sometimes by accepting and understanding what we would call bad or negative feelings, we can replace them with different feelings, allowing us to have more peace about the past.

Forgiving and reframing

An adult perspective on childhood experiences can allow us to see them in a new light, or to understand enough to forgive. A child may only see how a parent, for example, has let him down, without a mature understanding of the burdens that parent bore at the time. Adult reflection often allows us to realize our parents were doing the best they could under the circumstances, and to forgive them for what disappointed us so as children.

For example, we might bear a grudge about not getting some toy or pet or thing we wanted as children, or some experience or opportunity. It may simply be that our parents could not afford it, or that they had an adult understanding that it would not be good for us. We may harbor hurt feelings over what we perceived as unequal treatment of siblings, but there may be a logical explanation we just did not have or could not understand at the time.

Even when an adult analysis leaves us feeling let down, we can still resolve to forgive. Parents are stretched and stressed in ways that children may not grasp. They may be dealing with illness or incapacity or reduced income. Often they are attempting to care for their own elderly parents just when their children need them most. Sometimes, they are simply repeating the dysfunctional scripts they lived with as children, behaving as their models did. It may never have occurred to them that there is a different and better way to behave. Recognizing such circumstances later can help us to see their behavior in a new and more sympathetic light.

We know that this is more easily said than done. In writing this book together, the authors have revisited their own difficult recurring memories. One of us has dealt with a series of deaths in the household for which she feels more than the obvious and appropriate grief. When her spouse was stricken with a terminal illness, she threw herself into trying to prolong his life and ease his pain—and ultimately failed on both counts. She felt angry with him for partially causing his disease and for leaving her. But while that passed with time, a strong sense of guilt lingers—regret that she didn't try hard enough, did not pay enough attention to small clues and symptoms, let fatigue and depression impair her judgment. She recognizes that these feelings are irrational, but feelings trump reason. She is still struggling, years later, to reframe the memories and to grant herself forgiveness.

Atoning

Or, suppose our recurring bad feelings stem from our own behavior that we regret and are ashamed of. Perhaps we spoke hatefully to someone we love, or left someone hanging when they needed us, or lied about something to protect ourselves. Have we attempted to "make it right" or to atone in some way? Have we looked back to see if there were extenuating circumstances that can help us to forgive ourselves for what we did? If it's too late to make amends, can we pay the debt forward somehow? If we picked on or bullied others as children, for example, could we coach or mentor children now to make up for that? If we believe we failed our own children in some way, can we be there for our grandchildren? Even when our adult perspective cannot remove the hurt or injustice, we can still resolve to forgive ourselves, to do better going forward, and to move on.

Denial of forgiveness

Sometimes, we are not allowed forgiveness for our past transgressions. Some people harbor grudges for a lifetime, while others manage to get past tremendous neglect and abuse to be empathetic, loving, and wise. Why do you suppose we can react so differently to negative events? We suggest that the root of these different reactions is our sense of efficacy—whether we feel like victims or in control of our lives. Every bit of control we take in our lives is empowering, adds to our confidence, and makes us less helpless. If, on the other hand, we remain passive and allow things to happen to and to be done to us, we will remain in a childlike state of dependence. When adults whine and complain about what others have done or not done to or for them, they are literally acting childish. They are stuck in the passivity and helplessness of childhood.

A parent, spouse, child, or friend may repeatedly throw in our faces how we wronged them in the past—and they may be correct. If we have sincerely acknowledged fault, apologized, and attempted to atone, we may have done all we can. When someone refuses to give up a grudge, *they* must work it out. Silence or absence may be the best response, the only way to stop feeding their feelings. It may take the assistance of a trained therapist to break such a chain of recriminations.

Looking for the bright side

Beyond explaining, reframing, and forgiving, looking back may allow us to appreciate any "silver linings" that came with a relationship, illness, or experience. Ultimately, good things often result that would not have occurred otherwise. Age and time has a great way of bringing healing to past wounds, sadness, disappointments, and fears. We find it is especially crucial to search for some neutral or even good feelings when a relationship has ended, or when someone we cared about has moved away, or when a loved one has passed away. Holding on to bitterness after such losses hurts only us.

Emotions control our production of hormones, and they affect every system of our bodies. Our health is directly dependent on how we manage our emotions, so we had best learn to do so. Letting go of anger, hurt, and disappointment brings the peace that literally makes us feel better.

ENTRY 83

Is there a particular strong memory that recurs to trouble me? What happened and who else was involved? Looking back on it, might I have misinterpreted what happened? Can I find some way to better understand and tolerate the person whose behavior so upset me — even if that person was me?

_____

_____

_____

_____

_____

_____

_____

_____

ENTRY 84

If I find myself unable to forgive someone for something that happened long ago, why is that? Am I still blaming others for my own feelings — of regret, inadequacy, failure? Am I trying to avoid facing my own culpability in the matter?

_____

_____

_____

_____

_____

_____

_____

_____

_____

_____

_____

_____

ENTRY 85

If I still believe, after an adult reanalysis, that I was truly wronged, what shall I do about it? Did anything good come from this episode? Did the experience make me feel helpless in some way? How might I have stuck up for myself and asserted control? If I manage to forgive the person I blame, will my own life be better?

_____

_____

_____

_____

_____

_____

_____

_____

_____

_____

_____

_____

_____

_____

_____

_____

_____

_____

_____

_____

_____

_____

_____

_____

A Special Case: Feelings about Learning

We all realize nowadays that ongoing training and learning will be a given in our lives. We will be much happier and more successful at it after some introspection about our conscious and subconscious feelings about learning. Many of us have felt incapable, stressed, confused, pressured, angry, or resentful in classes or other learning experiences. We may have internalized the notion that we are "no good at" something, which prevents us from ever getting better at it.

One way to break such self-fulfilling prophecies of failure is to think about when you feel good about learning—whether it is about using a new cell phone or appliance, trying a new sport or hobby, or joining a team or formal class. When do you feel confident or capable? What kind of people are you with? What are the activities or ways in which you learn best?

Think back to a time when you learned something easily. Perhaps it was learning to whistle or to snap your fingers or to tie your shoes. These childhood experiences illustrate how we can make learning easier. First, it cannot happen unless we are willing to admit that we do not know something. This sounds self-evident, but thinking we know more than we do often hinders real learning. Second, easy and natural learning experiences were most likely low-stress ones: there were no time limits or grades or public judging of our efforts and results. Our teacher, probably mom or a sibling, was patient and willing — and probably cared about us. He or she encouraged us when we were frustrated and had confidence we would succeed. He or she probably taught mostly by modeling what to do and how. We weren't perfect at first, but

practiced either until something just clicked or until we slowly mastered a process. We learned in a kind of informal apprenticeship that responded to our individual needs and lasted just as long as needed.

This is exactly how almost all of us learned to speak our native languages —a feat so complex and difficult that many of us have never been able to repeat it to become fluent in a second language. Our seemingly effortless success at one and failure despite effort at the other give us insight into ways to make learning easier and more natural. Most importantly, they tell us that our learning failures are likely rooted not in *ourselves* or any inherent lack of ability, but rather in a flawed process. We need to try both better and harder: giving a learning project we care about the same persistent and confident effort that has worked for us before, and ditching the stress of deadlines, grades, and indifferent teachers whenever we can. If we try, it is not all that difficult to find someone who can teach us well and to allow him or her to do so. We need humility and openness as much as energy and dedication.

When we recognize there are myriad ways to learn just about anything— be it cooking, driving a car, starting a business, being a parent or grandparent, operating a piece of machinery, putting together a new gizmo, or starting a new healthy diet or fitness routine—we can be in charge of how, what, and when we will learn. We can overcome the barrier of negative feelings and set ourselves up to have a positive learning experience.

ENTRY 86

Many of us have been forced in today's economy to train for a new career. The prospect can fill us with terror. We expect to fail. We see our shortcomings but do not acknowledge our talents or skills. Have you experienced this fear and feeling of inadequacy? Can you realize how much more you know and can do than the last time you were in school? Do you recognize how much your desire, motivation, and determination can help you to learn now? Do you have more insight now about how you learn and what tools or resources you need to learn well?

_____

_____

_____

_____

_____

_____

Taking the Reins

We can take back control over our emotions! While we cannot prevent feelings from arising, we can control what we choose to do or not do, say or not say, about them. We may harness some of them by not going places, doing things, or being with people where negative feelings always seem to surface. On the other hand, we can recognize good, pleasurable, and healthy feelings and note what we were thinking, where we were, who we were with, and what we were doing when they arose. Then we can purposefully will ourselves to replicate these experiences and have more of these good and balanced feelings.

We can re-evaluate past experiences and find new interpretations of what happened. People who let us down may not have been as heartless or selfish as we once thought. Perhaps they were dealing, if poorly, with serious traumas of their own that we knew nothing about at the time. Even those who did the inexcusable can be forgiven, inside our hearts and minds, so that we may experience the relief of letting go. We can even strive to forgive ourselves for words or deeds we regret, perhaps making amends first or determining to pay a debt forward when we can no longer interact with those we wronged.

Good things *can* happen as a result of bad experiences; that's why "when one door closes, another opens" has become a cliché.

We can analyze our past relationships and experiences to understand how feelings arising from them are still driving us today in subconscious ways. We need not let feelings run us over or turn us into people we don't want to be. Feelings can be a great motivator to change our lives in productive ways. And we can choose to respond to the feelings of other people in our lives in effective, practical, healthy, and respectful ways.

Summary of Journey 3

Feelings are *always* part of my thinking, learning, and decisions.

Sensory triggers often evoke feelings without consciously arousing the memories of what caused them.

I cannot escape from a dysfunctional rut until I see that I am in it.

While I cannot prevent feelings, I can manage their expression.

Reinterpreting past experiences can change my feelings about them.

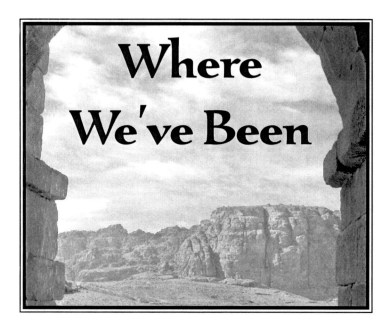

Where We've Been

By now, we have done a tremendous amount of careful reflection upon our life experiences. We have a much better idea of who and what made us into the persons we are today.

We understand that our true beliefs and values and the origins of our feelings may be mysteriously hidden in our subconscious minds, even though they guide and impel our actions. But recognizing what really drives us is the beginning of being able to change, to take back the tiller to steer our lives in the direction we want to go.

We can choose new beliefs and values to live by. We can break the hold of old feelings and childhood roles. We can establish new habit patterns that serve us better. We can judiciously decide to alter our path and even to change our companions on the journey.

We now have an idea how to strike a balance between taking control of our lives and appropriately ceding control to support relationships that bring us joy. We know that finding the happy medium—between independence and interdependence, between vulnerability and security—is the task of a lifetime.

Now that we have brought feelings, values, and assumptions to conscious awareness, we are equipped to override and discard those that no longer fit our conception of who we want to become and where we choose to go.

Summary of Our Journeys

My value as a person comes from my values.

I choose my beliefs and values—and can change them.

My actions demonstrate my true beliefs and values.

Relationships are not lasting and satisfying
unless they are reciprocal.

Understanding my feelings robs them
of the power to control me.

Reflection allows experience to become wisdom.

Bon Voyage!

About the Authors

For over 20 years, the authors have created and managed mentoring programs for children and teens and helped other organizations to do the same. This book distills the learning, training, reflection, and discussions that we developed to build effective mentors. In designing programs, we defined a few key questions for our youth to answer:

Who am I? Who do I want to become?

What do I believe in and value? Do my actions reflect my beliefs and values?

Will I leave a legacy to be proud of?

We wanted teens to analyze and define themselves in order to set a new direction for their lives. But a stark reality hit home every time we began training our volunteer mentors: most adults were hard pressed to answer these very questions. Many confessed that they were hardly in control of or happy with their own lives. They had long ago given up on some goals and dreams. They were immersed in trying to keep up with hectic schedules and diverse responsibilities. They lacked balance or a sense of purpose.

Many of us have never considered these key questions, which are the foundation that allows for a satisfying life. We are so busy *doing* that we forget to ask what we are doing and why. *Passport 2 Purpose* urges us to take the time to reflect upon our life journey, to analyze where we have come from and want to go, what is holding us back or taking us off course.

We will guide you through discovering your hidden motivations — subconscious emotional drivers rooted in your past. Many of our instinctive reactions stem from painful experiences earlier in life, so we don't really like to bring them into conscious awareness. But growth usually comes from pain: that is when we are receptive to learning because we realize that we don't know everything. Recognizing, understanding, and managing our feelings can put us back in control of our lives.

Whether or not you have any interest in mentoring programs, recognize that we are all mentors and mentees. Every parent and child, coworker or colleague, friend or neighbor learns from others and serves as a role model to them. Why not play your roles with deliberate, well-thought-out intent?

While *Michigan Reach Out* no longer runs active mentoring programs, we do offer workshop retreats based upon *Passport 2 Purpose*. Visit us at
www.passport-2-purpose.org.

CPSIA information can be obtained at www.ICGtesting.com
Printed in the USA
BVOW060902081211

277887BV00004B/6/P